Healing the Unhealed Mind

Healing the Unhealed Mind

THE PRACTICE OF *A COURSE IN MIRACLES*

KENNETH WAPNICK, PH.D.

Foundation for A Course in Miracles®

Foundation for A COURSE IN MIRACLES®
41397 Buecking Drive
Temecula, CA 92590
www.facim.org

Copyright 2011 by the
Foundation for A COURSE IN MIRACLES®

First printing, 2011

Printed in the United States of America

Library of Congress Cataloging-in-Publication Data

Wapnick, Kenneth, 1942-
   Healing the unhealed mind / Kenneth Wapnick.
       p. cm.
   Includes index.
   ISBN 978-1-59142-546-5
  1. Course in Miracles. 2. Spiritual life. 3. Spiritual healing.
   4. Mind and body therapies--Miscellanea. I. Title.
   BP605.C68W3536 2011
   299'.93--dc23

                            2011041662

CONTENTS

Preface

This latest title in our series "The Practice of *A Course in Miracles*" is largely based on my 2009 seminar entitled "The Unhealed Healer." It reflects the theme of *mind and body* that I repeatedly come back to in my teaching. It is also directly related to a weekend workshop I gave in 1990 in our former location in Roscoe, New York. Entitled "Healing the Unhealed Healer," that workshop provided a line-by-line commentary on the section in the text, "The Unhealed Healer" (T-9.V). In the 2009 seminar, I referred to that interesting section, but focused more on the relationship between mind and body, rather than the actual material in the text.

The theme of *mind and body* can be restated as the theme of *form and content* that is so often discussed in *A Course in Miracles*. The ego preserves itself by having us identify with the external or physical form at the expense of the mind's content. In the context of this book, we see the ego's ingenuity in having us focus on the external symptoms of sickness, their amelioration being seen as healing. True healing, however, comes only when we let the true Healer return our attention to the mind's symptom of guilt.

By so doing, our unhealed minds are cleansed of the erroneous belief in guilt's reality, freeing us to become healed healers.

The ego, the part of us that likes being separated and special, fears the power of the mind to recognize its original and ongoing mistake of choosing the ego as its teacher instead of the Holy Spirit. To defend against the mind correcting itself, which signifies the end of the ego and individual existence, it carries out its strategy of mindlessness. By making a world (macrocosmically) and a body (microcosmically), and then causing us to forget what it did, it renders us all mindless creatures, without any hope of the true salvation that comes when we return to our minds and choose again.

The current book includes questions and answers from the earlier workshop, several from the seminar, a question from the 2010 Academy class, "The Way to Remember God," and a series of questions on a common theme from the 2006 Academy class, "The Imperfection in the Godhead: Fact or Fiction?" In fact, all of Part II of the book consists of these questions, which allowed for a more in-depth discussion of a theme that is absolutely central to the teaching of *A Course in Miracles*, a theme that can be succinctly summarized as follows: the mind is not in the body; the body is in the mind. This reflects the all-important principle of *ideas leave not their source* and is the basis for true healing. When this principle is not recognized and understood, the mistake known as *making the error real* becomes inevitable. The healer's focus has shifted from the mind to the body, making healing impossible since only the mind needs to be healed, since only the mind is sick. Our recognizing that sickness and healing are only of the mind is one of the Course's major purposes, for it is the basis of forgiveness. It is the purpose of this book to help further students' understanding of this process, which is a significant part of the healing journey we take with Jesus.

We have followed our usual practice in this series of editing the excerpts to enhance readability, but never so much that the informal, spontaneous flavor of the classes is lost. It is always a challenge to stay on the right side of the fine line that divides the formal and informal, and we hope we have succeeded here.

As with all the books in this series, "The Practice of *A Course in Miracles*," I hope that *Healing the Unhealed Mind* will be efficacious in the process of students of *A Course in Miracles* choosing to heal their minds, allowing them to become healed healers, extending the healing love that they have now accepted for themselves.

Acknowledgments

I am deeply grateful to Rosemarie LoSasso, the Foundation's Director of Publications for so many years, who once again demonstrated her remarkable ability to knit together parts of various workshops into a whole that presents a unified theme. She, as always, faithfully nursed the book from a concept into the finished product you now hold in your hands.

I have commented earlier in this series on my wife Gloria's inspiration that led to this series of small books. My gratitude for this extends even more specifically to *Healing the Unhealed Mind*, for after attending the aforementioned 2009 seminar, Gloria insisted we put it out as book. Other projects unfortunately took precedence, but I am pleased that Gloria's insistence has finally led to the book's publication. I remain forever grateful for her perceptive and insightful editorial work that helps ensure the quality of this and my other books. Gloria has been my faithful and loving partner not only through thirty years of marriage but also in our joint direction of the Foundation, which has existed almost as long. She was not only the Foundation's inspiration, but has been its guiding light from its small beginnings in a converted one-car garage to the present day.

Part One

1. Introduction

"The Unhealed Healer," the original title of the workshop on which this book is based, is also the title of a section in Chapter 9 in the text. Interestingly, it is the only place in *A Course in Miracles* where Jesus talks specifically about something other than the Course's primary focus on the mind's guilt and forgiveness. He speaks of psychotherapists and theologians, using each as an example of the ego's plan of forgiveness, one of the major themes of Chapter 9. The preceding section, in fact, is called "The Holy Spirit's Plan of Forgiveness." Jesus uses those two disciplines, psychotherapy and theology, as a way of demonstrating the mistake known as *making the error real*. If the Course believed in sin, that would be a sin.

Both these disciplines have as their purpose to help, but they ultimately become part of the problem. The therapist is supposed to heal the mind or psyche, but *mind* is not thought of the way the Course means it. We will discuss that later. A therapist would say that the contents of the psyche are real and are horrific. Psychotherapy, in the context of this discussion, is psychoanalytic psychotherapy. (That is the only form of therapy Helen Schucman was trained in and really knew. Remember, she was scribing the Course in the 1960s, before the current plethora of therapeutic modalities emerged.) The error lies in making the contents of the unconscious or psyche real, and then trying to do something about it.

Theologians, and people in religious life in general, try to heal us of our sin and reunite us with God. In this context, the error is in making sin real. While *A Course in Miracles* in one sense talks about the ego system as being based on original sin, it teaches unequivocally that sin never happened. The *belief* in sin, over what never occurred in reality, is the problem. We will come back to that also. Certainly in the biblical religions, Judaism and the many differing forms of Christianity, original sin is taken as an ontological reality. In the Bible, you may recall, sin is so much of a reality that God Himself responds to it. You simply have to read Chapter 3 in Genesis to see God's angry response. The sin against the Creator (Adam and Eve's disobedience; i.e., the separation from, and opposition to, God's Will) is very real, with disastrous consequences.

The brunt of this section in the text, which goes to the heart of the entire Course, centers on making the ego thought system real, with all the ramifications, permutations, and combinations of that original mistake of believing we are separate from our Source. Consequently, anything we do to undo the ego thought system of separation that we have first made real, the Course calls "magic." This would include all special relationships, all the ways we make the body real, all the ways we make our relationships with other bodies real, whether they are sources of pleasure or pain—all these are but different forms of defending against the underlying premise that the separation from God and His Love actually occurred.

The correction for that (I am basically giving you an overview here; we shall go into greater depth later) is not being concerned with the forms that sin has taken, because they are not the problem. The problem is that we as decision-making minds have made the sin real. That is why there is *no order of difficulty in miracles*. Every miracle, which of course has nothing to do with anything external, is the mind's correction for its belief that the separation from God is a fact. That we have expressed this belief in billions and billions of forms does not matter. None of these is the problem. This is why Jesus repeatedly says that his is a simple course. In fact, the first section of the last chapter of the text is called "The Simplicity of Salvation" (T-31.I). What is true is true, what is false is false, and there is nothing else to discuss. The meaning of applying this course to our everyday life, the purpose of developing a relationship with Jesus, the Holy Spirit, or any other symbol of a non-ego presence in our minds, is to have us return to the mind so we can re-examine the original belief that the separation was an actual event. If that original belief is not challenged and undone, we become unhealed healers and nothing we do will help. This is why we say that the minds of therapist and theologian are unhealed, for they have not accepted within themselves the fact that the separation is an illusion. Everything they do cannot help but be contaminated by that false belief, which directly interferes with their healing work.

2. Form and Content

What the "Unhealed Healer" section is about, not to mention this workshop and *A Course in Miracles* itself, is getting past the form to the content. *Form and content* is a major theme in this course. *Form* is anything that has to do with behavior, anything that occurs in the material universe, which includes the entire cosmos: our galaxy, the galaxies beyond this galaxy, anything that has materiality—in a phrase, the entire phenomenal universe. *Form*, therefore, is any *thing* in the world. This includes the personal world, which we think of as our individual lives that begin with conception, then birth, and the various developmental stages up to and including death. In other words, anything the body thinks, feels, says, and does.

Content is only of the mind, and the content of the mind has only two components: the ego thought system of guilt, sin, fear, attack, judgment, and death, and the Holy Spirit's correction thought system of forgiveness, healing, peace, and love. Those are the only two contents. Again, that is why Jesus tells us this is all very simple. There are even some places where he says this is easy, at which point most of us would, if we have not already done so, throw the book at him. I remember once many, many years ago, probably long before any of you were born, someone wrote to us and said, "I just thought you would want to know how long it takes to flush the Course down the toilet bowl." He told us, but he did not tell us what his plumbing bills were, because at that point the Course consisted of three hardcover volumes.

At any rate, it certainly does not *feel* easy. What does makes it easy, though, is recognizing there is only one problem and one solution, as the workbook says in Lesson 80 (W-pI.80.3:5). When you finally get that, everything becomes really easy. Your entire life becomes easy. Even the most tragic things that may occur to you or to people in your personal life or even in the world—even what the world would consider the most tragic things—will be seen easily, and you will get by all the pain very easily when you recognize that nothing on the level of form is the problem; nothing on the level of the body is the problem. When *A Course in Miracles* talks about the body, it is always talking about the physical body *and* the psychological body. The distinction is never really made, but as you read the Course you recognize that it is talking not only about the physical experience of pain, but also the psychological or emotional experience of pain. Once again, nothing of the body is the problem.

In fact whatever we experience in the body is a distraction from the real problem: the mind's decision for the wrong teacher.

One Problem – One Solution

This takes us back to the very beginning when the tiny, mad idea seemed to arise in the mind of God's Son; the tiny, mad idea that God's Son could be separate from his Source Who is perfect Oneness and perfect Love. Obviously, if separation from perfect Oneness were possible, perfect Oneness would no longer be perfect Oneness. And if there is no perfect Oneness, there can be no God. In *A Course in Miracles*, God is defined as perfect Oneness, Love, and Wholeness, which means that His essence and reality as pure spirit is undivided, unseparated, undifferentiated, and perfectly whole, as is His one Son. As one workbook lesson says, "…nowhere does the Father end, the Son begin as something separate from Him" (W-pI.132.12:4).

Logically following from this (and the Course's thought system is very logical), terms such as *Father and Son, God and Christ, cause and effect* have no

meaning. These are dualistic concepts that are meaningful to us who live in a dualistic world in which the
concept of parent and child is very close to us. That is
not the case in Heaven. I like to point out that even
though the Course uses Trinitarian language—Father,
Son, and Holy Spirit, where the Son is not Jesus but
Christ, all of us—it says quite clearly there is no Trinity because "[God] is the First in the Holy Trinity
Itself" (T-7.I.7:5) and there is no second and no third.
Perfect Oneness cannot have a second and a third. Thus
in truth there is no Trinity, no place where the Father
ends and the Son begins as something separate from
Him—the state of perfect Oneness.

The *tiny, mad idea* that we could be separate from
our Creator and Source therefore is impossible, but
once that idea seemed to have arisen in the mind, we
took it seriously, the "we" being the collective and
separated Son. This is before there was a world of differentiation and fragmentation. There was only one
Son who believed, in the delusional thought system of
his insanity, that he had separated from his Source.
That belief, however, cannot be the problem, because
it never happened. How could what never happened—because it *could not* happen—be a problem?
The problem is we believed it happened, which means
it is not the thought of separation that is the problem;

it is the *belief* in it. Once we believed it happened, as one passage near the end of Chapter 27 points out, we made it a very serious occurrence (T-27.VIII.6:3). We gave it a name, the most serious name one can give anything in this world: *sin*. Something horrifically and horrendously horrible happened. We took perfect Oneness and destroyed it. And all because we believed we existed, and wanted that existence no matter what the cost, and to Whom.

This is the beginning of the Course's mythology. It is important to understand that this is a myth. It is describing something that never happened, but it is describing it in a way we can relate to, because understanding what the original mistake was helps us deal with all the mistakes in our everyday life. If this course cannot be lived, if its principles cannot be practiced and applied, it means nothing. The myth is necessary only in providing a framework within which we can make sense of what is inherently an insane and a literally nonsensical life.

How could a life outside Heaven be meaningful? Everything here is inherently meaningless because it is separated from true Meaning. That is what the early workbook lessons mean, beginning with the first lesson that teaches that nothing in this world means anything. Nothing in this world means anything because this is a meaningless world. Now it does have the meaning that the Holy Spirit gives it, which we will discuss below. This is that the world is a classroom. But in itself the world is inherently meaningless because it has been erected (or miscreated) upon a thought that is itself meaningless, being separate from true Meaning.

The problem, again, is that we took it seriously. We said the separation actually happened, and not only did it actually happen, but it had very real effects. The real effects of that *tiny, mad idea* of being separate from our Source are everything that goes on in this world. The cosmos is the effect on a macrocosmic level, and on a microcosmic level the body is the effect. The problem is not the *tiny, mad idea*. The problem is not the so-called sin against God, the shattering of perfect Oneness. It is not the crucifixion of God's Son, which incidentally became the foundation for the Christian myth that we crucified Christ (the Course's name for God's Son). The problem is none of these. *The problem is that we believed in it and thought it actually occurred.*

This distinction is crucial because it goes to the heart of the unhealed healer's situation. The unhealed healer believes there is a problem. For all his brilliance and genius, Freud missed this very important point. In fact one can say that even though he was an atheist, he studied this "problem" religiously. The problem of guilt never happened, but he thought it was real. No one described with more insight than he how the ego worked, what he called the psyche or unconscious. Except there was nothing there to work!

Many of you have heard me quote what Jesus said to Helen when she was taking the Course down (Helen was basically a Freudian, as was Bill): "Freud knew a bad thing when he perceived it; he just did not know that bad things do not exist." That one line is a perfect summary of Freud's creative brilliance and vast contribution, and yet his very limited view of the mind. He knew the bad thing when he saw it; he knew the ego thought system inside and out. He just did not know that there was no ego thought system, which is why the Course says that we do not have to analyze the ego. There is an important line that says, "The ego analyzes; the Holy Spirit accepts" (T-11.V.13:1). The ego analyzes, studies, and tries to make sense of itself. All the Holy Spirit does is accept that an illusion is an illusion is an illusion, being nothing but a flimsy veil that hides the truth about our reality. There is one passage that is meant as a critique of the practice of psychoanalysis, where Jesus says we do not have to follow "all the circuitous routes" that the ego thought system takes (T-15.X.5:1), which is exactly what Freud did.

This, then, is the burden of the section, "The Unhealed Healer." What makes us unhealed healers is that we do not recognize that what has to be healed, changed, or understood is not the ego. *What has to be healed is the mind's belief in the ego*. That distinction is not a subtle one, and needs to be reinforced continually in our awareness. This entire course rests on understanding that distinction. It is the meaning of this line that most students of *A Course in Miracles* know very well: "Therefore, seek not to change the world, but choose to change your mind about the world" (T-21.in.1:7). The problem is not the world. How can what does not exist, because it comes from a thought that does not exist, be a problem? The problem is that we believe it exists, and that belief is in the decision-making mind. The Course never uses the term *decision maker*, except in one reference that says the body is not the decision maker (see M-5.II.1:7). But it is a helpful term to point to the part of the mind that is always choosing between the ego's interpretation of the *tiny, mad idea* and the Holy Spirit's or Jesus' interpretation. That is the role of the decision maker.

As one Son we collectively decided wrongly. We believed the ego's lie, the lie that said the separation from God happened. And once we believed it, we were off and running, having to defend against it and ultimately make up a world, and then the body, as the ultimate defense against the consequences of sin. And of these, the primary consequence is that we deserve to be punished.

The third chapter of Genesis is a wonderful depiction of the birth of the ego. When we read it, it should be obvious that in no way can *A Course in Miracles* and the Bible be made compatible. Everything in the Bible from that point on, to the Book of Revelation at the end of the New Testament, is based on that third chapter, which gives the account of Adam and Eve eating of the forbidden fruit (it never says it was an apple, by the way). They then become aware that God is walking in the garden and are terrified that He will punish them. Out of their sense of guilt over having disobeyed God, they hide in the bushes so He will not find them. They cover their private parts because they immediately associate their sin with sexuality, from which Christianity derived its insane thought of linking sexuality and sin. Then God finds them. The rest of that chapter, which so many people think is

actually theologically correct, deals with God's punishment: His sinful children will henceforth suffer and
die, their children will be born in pain, and on and on.
There was no death until God caught up with the two
sinners. To make things even worse, God banishes
them forever from the garden. He kicks them out of
Heaven, and then has angels with flaming and circling
spears ensure that they will never get back. The rest of
the Bible, Old and New Testament alike, is built on
sin and God's insane plan for the salvation of His
people, who are descendants of these two original
sinners.

Whatever you may think of the Bible, please do
not say it is like the Course, or that the Course is like
the Bible. They are apples and pears; better even,
apples and spinach since they are not even the same
species. That chapter in Genesis says that the belief in
the separation from God's Will really happened, and
was such a serious event that God noticed it. This is
the telling thing. God noticed the sin and took it so
seriously that He went on the warpath. As I like to
point out, if you are looking for the prototype of an
over-reaction, you will find it par excellence in the
biblical God. He clearly over-reacts. The most
abusive father in the world does not hold a candle to
God and His wrath, and it is all over nothing. It is God

Who has the authority problem. His authority is challenged and He gets even. Therefore, never mess with those with power because when they feel their authority is challenged they will use it against you. The prototype, once again, is God.

This is all based upon the belief that the separation from God, called *sin*, actually happened and was serious. However, the reality is that we never separated from God. This is what *A Course in Miracles* calls the principle of the Atonement, which is the Holy Spirit's correction principle, found in the right mind. Remember, at this point in our myth there is no world, no body, no brain. Please do not make a connection between the wrong and the right mind, and the left and right brain. They have nothing to do with each other. One can be left-brained and right-minded, and wrong-minded and right-brained. The mind and brain have nothing to do with anything; the brain is not the mind and the mind is not the brain, though its decisions are reflected there.

The problem is that we took the separation seriously and then believed God was going to punish us for having enacted it. Therefore, in order to escape from His wrath, totally nonexistent of course, we made up a world in which we could hide, a world that is the opposite of Heaven. Thus, everything Heaven is, the world is not. Heaven is unchanging and undifferentiated, the eternal home of perfect Love, Oneness, and Wholeness. Everything here is exactly the opposite, for the ego self is the opposite of the glorious Self that God created.

Having made up this world, magically believing we could hide from God there, we fragmented ourselves into billions and billions of pieces, each one being housed in a body. Our discussion will remain with homo sapiens, although this would work for any other material form in the universe. From that point on, the body became the way of defending against the mind, wherein God would destroy us. In other words, the mind became a battleground in which we found ourselves at war with God. Remember, the true God knows nothing of this. We hide from God by *seemingly* escaping into a world and a body. The body, the home of the special relationship, then becomes the principal means of defending against God's wrath. We displace our belief in the wrath of God onto everyone else. This is why the Course says the authority problem "*is* 'the root of all evil'" (T-3.VI.7:3), not money, as the Bible says. The authority problem is originally with God, and then is displaced onto every other authority in our lives.

The problem, however, is never with anyone here, because the problem is never with God. There is no God Who is angry, Who has been sinned against. There is only a God of Love and Oneness, Whose reality is not even far beyond this world, for His Being has nothing to do with this world at all. This is why Jesus says that love is not possible here (T-4.III.4), where love is always expressed from one person to another, or one person to an object, substance, activity, cause, or book—especially if it has a blue cover. That is not love. It cannot be love if it is from one person to another, for that is duality. Love is non-dualistic Oneness. What is possible in the world, as the Course says, is to reflect Heaven's Love, which is the meaning of forgiveness (e.g., W-pI.46; W-pI.60.1).

Again, we made the world and the body to be a defense against a thought that never happened. When you realize that, you understand why Jesus over and over again in his teaching says that we should laugh and have a gentle smile; we should take nothing in this world seriously in the sense that it has power over us. We should do this because the world was literally made as a defense against something that never happened, which is just plain silly. One of the greatest jokes in the history of the world is that we call human beings *homo sapiens*, which means "wise man"

("man" in the generic sense of species, not gender). How could we be wise when we continue to try to solve the problem of the body and the world when neither exists, when both were made to defend against a thought that does not exist, and against a God that does not exist? That is hardly wise, yet in the arrogance of the ego we call ourselves *homo sapiens*.

Those of you who know Jonathan Swift's brilliant satire *Gulliver's Travels,* will recall that he made the wise species the horse, which he called Houyhnhnms. Homo sapiens became Yahoos—the origin of *yahoo.com*—creatures who did not know anything. But *we* think we know. We actually think we understand what the world is. We think we understand the meaning of our lives. We think we understand how to gain pleasure and avoid pain, how to achieve happiness and success here. And there are so many wise brains telling us how to do it. Yet none of them knows anything at all for they believe in the reality of what does not exist.

The only way we can find real peace, and have real pleasure and happiness is to return to our minds and choose again: the teacher of sanity instead of the teacher of insanity; the teacher of the gentle laugh, not the teacher who is so serious about illusions. To apply this thought in our everyday life, we need to see how seriously we take everything that goes on here: how seriously we take the news, what goes on in our personal lives—our jobs, families, and bodies—our pursuit of goals where we actually believe that attaining them will bring us something that we need and want.

The only value this world has, and the only value our bodies and our experiences have is that they are classrooms in which we learn that we are minds and not bodies, that we inhabit the world of thoughts of the mind, not the seeming world of external reality. That is the only value. The reason this course is typically not for young people is that we usually spend the first part of our lives learning how to master the world and our bodies; how to attain pleasure and avoid pain; how to form relationships with other bodies; sometimes to have families, acquire an education, get jobs, and so on. All of this is very important in order to survive in the world.

A person cannot do all that, however, while at the same time believing the world is an illusion. Thus, it is usually not until we are a little farther along in our lives—at least in our 30s typically, but it could be later or earlier—that we suddenly realize, as the workbook says, "The world I see holds nothing that I want" (W-pI.128). We recognize how insane this world is, how nothing here works for too long: relationships, bodies, automobiles, computers, governments, the stock market, and the weather. Nothing works! The world cannot work because it comes from an insane thought that does not work.

3. Projection Makes Perception

One of the key dynamics to understand in this course is projection. Many of you may have heard me say that when Helen was taking the Course down from Jesus, he said to her and Bill that the only value in their being psychologists, for the purposes of learning *A Course in Miracles,* was that they understood projection. *Projection* is the psychological term for the dynamic of taking something we find unacceptable in our mind and getting rid of it by projecting it out, magically believing that now it is no longer in us but in someone or something else. For instance, if I feel guilty about something, and guilt always ends up being unconscious because we repress it, I seek to get rid of it by seeing the trait I find unacceptable in me in another. I then attack and judge that person. I wake up every morning lusting after a sinner so I can make a judgment I can justify. And all that I am doing is saying the sin is out there and not in me.

This is the meaning of the workbook line:

> When you feel that you are tempted to accuse someone of sin in any form, do not allow your mind to dwell on what you think he did, for that

is self-deception. Ask instead, "Would I accuse myself of doing this?" (W-pI.134.9:2-3).

This is not always true on the level of form, but it is always true on the level of content. If you have chosen Jesus as your teacher and feel the ongoing presence of his love, you can never have a judgmental thought about anyone—impossible. Why? The answer lies in another principle based on projection that is so important it is said twice in the text: "Projection makes perception" (T-13.V.3:5; T-21.in.1:1). I first look within my mind, choose the teacher whose thought system I espouse and identify with, and then project or extend the guilt or love I have chosen, perceiving it in the world. If it is from the right mind, I will *extend* it, but since the dynamic is the same, we will sometimes stay with the word *projection* for convenience.

Thus, if I have chosen Jesus as my teacher and experience his love and peace, I will project that out, seeing love and peace all around me. If people are not living in a peaceful, loving way, I will understand that they are really afraid of the love that is in them, and I will hear the fear, not the attack. Jesus tells us early in the text that "frightened people can be vicious" (T-3.I.4:2), and so through Christ's vision I understand that people's viciousness is coming from their fear. Since I am, in this holy instant of sanity, filled with the reflection of the Love of God, I will embrace people with that love, which I cannot do if I see them as attacking, being vicious or unkind. I can embrace them in my mind only if I realize that their attack is coming from their fear. What is a loving brother to do but embrace them in that love, which is automatic once I choose the teacher of love? There is that wonderful lesson that says, "I feel the Love of God within me now" (W-pI.209.1:1). When I feel that love I cannot attack, which means that when I find myself attacking, judging, criticizing, or finding fault, it must be because I am no longer choosing the teacher of love, but the teacher of guilt instead. It has to be that, and this mistaken decision *is* my problem, not anything external, regardless of its form.

Perception in the Course always means *the mind's interpretation* of what the physical eyes see. What I perceive must come from what I have first made real in my mind because *projection makes perception*. There are many fundamental premises that underlie the Course's thought system which, if you do not agree with them, would suggest that *A Course in Miracles* is not your path. The Course says it is only one path among many thousands (M-1.4:2), so there are many, many more you can choose from. But this course will not work for you if you do not accept certain basic premises. One of these is *projection makes perception*, which itself is based on a more basic premise that says the world is not real and so is not there, except in dreams.

Why is the world not there? This is where a principle parallel to *projection makes perception* comes in: *ideas leave not their source* (see, for example, T-26.VII.4:7; W-pI.132.5:3). This principle says that the idea of separation, or the idea of guilt can never leave its source in the mind and be projected out to make a world. This is why the Course says "There is no world!" and means it literally (W-pI.132.6:2). There are many passages in this course that are not meant to be taken literally, such as God weeps, or God is incomplete without us. These are meant metaphorically. We are even told in the workbook to ask God and He will tell us what to do, when clearly He does not even know about us. This too, then, is meant metaphorically.* But again, the statement that there is no world is meant literally because *ideas leave not their source.*

---

* See my "Duality As Metaphor in *A Course in Miracles*," available in CD/Mp3 formats.

So, if nothing is out there, what are we respond-
ing to? It must be a projection of our minds, first on
the collective level (the world that we all made up
together), and then on a personal level (whatever we
feel gets us upset, makes us angry, depressed, fearful, sick, happy, joyful, or ecstatic). Anything that
we believe affects us (the mind) from the world is
untrue.

That is why the world is not to be taken seriously.
This is not to say that terrible things do not happen
here, because they clearly do, or that we should not do
things in this world. Jesus never tells us we should be
passive. He simply says we should be passive to the
ego and not do things on our own. In fact, many, many
times Jesus told Helen not to do anything without asking him first, and some of these statements were kept
in the text. What this means is that we should not do
anything in this world if we are coming from guilt. If
we are not asking Jesus for help, or not asking the
Holy Spirit to be our Teacher, we must be coming
from guilt for we are re-enacting the original moment
when we told God to get lost, saying: "Your Love is
not enough for me. The Self You created as one with
You is not enough. The world of Heaven, the world of
perfect Oneness is not what I want to be my home. I

will therefore leave You and make my own self, my own love, my own world." We did this first as a thought, and then after the great projection we did so as a physical experience. It is this madness that we re-enact each and every time we choose the teacher of guilt instead of the teacher of forgiveness.

The Principle of "Nothing Happened"

We do not have to ask help of Jesus or the Holy Spirit specifically. They are only symbols of a right-minded, non-judgmental, non-ego thought system or presence in our mind. Although *A Course in Miracles* uses only those two symbols, any other would work as well, since what matters is the source behind the symbol. What is important, however, is that we go to that symbol whenever tempted by our specialness to be angry, guilty, depressed, anxious, sick, despairing, resentful, and so on. This is where this course becomes practical.

We take as our model the response to the *tiny, mad idea* from the ego's point of view and the Holy Spirit's. The ego responds with "Isn't that wonderful!": serious, sinful, guilt-inducing, engendering fear if not terror, but still wonderful because we are on our own, and separated, autonomous, and free. The Holy Spirit's response to the *tiny, mad idea* is "What *tiny, mad idea*? What are you asking me about? There is nothing here. Nothing happened." The Holy Spirit is the great principle of the Nothing Happened. Nothing happened to disturb the perfect love of God's perfect Son: "…not one note in Heaven's song was missed" (T-26.V.5:4). That is the principle of the Nothing Happened. It seemed to have happened, and in the world of dreams it did happen. But dreams are not reality. Nothing came between God and His perfect Son. "Not one note in Heaven's song was missed." This principle of the Nothing Happened is the Atonement.

Whenever as individuals we choose not to experience the peace of God, a peace that embraces everyone as one, we are saying there is no Nothing Happened. This great principle of healing becomes Something Happened—something palpable and tangible, so real that it had consequences. We lie to ourselves each and every time we let anything in the world affect us, making us happy or sad; each and every time we give anything in the world power to give us pleasure or inflict pain, to cause us to go up or down emotionally. In all of this we are saying that there is a world out there, a body that the world impinges on, and that we are mindless and helpless creatures. And so if there is no mind, there is no God, because God is the memory in the mind, the memory that links us back to the Love we never left.

The purpose of this course is to have us understand this well enough that we can begin to apply it. It is the specific purpose of the workbook and its 365 lessons to train our minds to think the way Jesus thinks. He does not help us in the world, for how can he help us in a world that does not exist? Only a madman would do that. Only a madman would believe that God would intervene in a world that is not there. How could He? Psychotic people do that. Following this reasoning, it is clear that the God of the Bible is psychotic, as is His Son because *ideas leave not their source.* In Their delusional states They actually think there is a world of sin that needs saving, which means through the body. Again, please do not confuse the teachings in the Bible, which is one spiritual path, with the teachings of *A Course in Miracles*, which is another path entirely. Both will lead you home if you follow them with diligence and fidelity, but they are different. "Truth is one," the Hindus say, "the sages know it by many names." We want a teacher who is sane, not insane as we are, one who knows the difference between appearance and reality; a teacher who reminds us that we have a mind and that we can always choose again.

4. What It Means to Have a Mind:
Unhealed or Healed

One of the major problems to confront students who study this course is that they do not know what a mind is. Brain-mind researchers do not know what a mind is either, at least from the point of view of the Course. Almost always, with very few exceptions, when people write about the mind they are talking about an imperceptible activity of the brain. They say that the brain is a physical organ, but the mind is the activity of the brain that cannot be measured under a microscope. That is not how *A Course in Miracles* sees it at all. The problem for us is that the mind does not exist in a world of time and space. It is atemporal and non-spatial. Quantum physicists use the term *non-local*—the mind cannot be localized in a place. So often I get asked, "Where is the mind?" And that would seem a perfectly natural question to ask, but it cannot be answered because "where" presupposes space. The world of time and space came about as a projection of the thought system of the wrong mind, and it has never left its source. Recall that projection does not work, for what seems to be outside remains within.

4. What It Means to Have a Mind

The confusion in talking about the mind is that we do not know how to. The Course tells us that "God does not understand words, for they were made by separated minds to keep them in the illusion of separation" (M-21.1:7). Words were also made to keep us separate from the mind. The mind does not have words. We talk about Jesus being in the mind, but in the mind there is no Jesus. There is no specific person with a name. We talk about the Holy Spirit as a Teacher, as we do all the time, but in truth there is no person in the mind, which is abstract and non-specific. Lesson 161 says that "complete abstraction is the natural condition of the mind" (W-pI.161.2:1). Since the mind is non-specific, it is very difficult for specific brains to talk about it.

What we can do, however, is use metaphors. One I use all the time is of a child at a puppet show. The child thinks the puppets are real, while the adult understands that what is happening on the stage is not happening to a person. The puppet is totally make-believe, a non-living piece of wood or plastic that is dressed up and made by an unseen puppeteer to walk, talk, fall down, attack, be attacked, and so on. A small child does not know that, and so may become upset when its favorite puppet gets hurt. As adults we do not become upset because we understand the difference between the unseen puppeteer and the puppet.

The puppeteer is the mind, and the puppet is the world. The section called "The Laws of Chaos" in Chapter 23 is one of the more difficult sections in the text to work with. In fact it is the only section that has very little that is good in it. In most sections in the text, the first half is about the ego; the second half is the Holy Spirit's happy correction. Not so in "The Laws of Chaos." It begins with hell, takes us through hell, and virtually leaves us in hell. After the five laws of chaos are described in painfully graphic detail, which is a summary of the ego thought system, Jesus continues. You think it cannot get any worse, and then it does: "Can you paint rosy lips upon a skeleton ... pet it and pamper it, and make it live?" (T-23.II.18:8).

The skeleton represents the body, and Jesus is not attacking women who put on lipstick. That is just a symbol. Yet we all take something that is essentially lifeless and think it is alive. We think the puppet talks. That happens only in "The Twilight Zone," not in this world where puppets do not talk. There are many passages in all three books—text, workbook, manual—that tell us that the body does not do anything; eyes do not see, ears do not hear, brains do not think; bodies are not born, they do not die, they do not get sick, they do not get well; they do not attack or make decisions. Bodies simply follow what the mind tells them to do. (See for example, T-19.IV-C.5; T-28.V.4, VI.2.)

Another useful metaphor is that of a computer. A computer cannot do anything without a program, which is written by programmers who are not in your office or in your computer. They are unseen, but what they write will dictate what your computer does. If they write a program that says two and two is seven, then every time you strike 2 + 2 you will get 7. If for some perverse reason they write a program that says when you type A you will get E, then every time you strike A you will see E on your screen, no matter how many times you do it. That is what your computer has been told to do. Until you change the program, 2 + 2 will always equal 7, and every time you strike an A it will be an E. And all the while you do not see the programmers.

Accordingly, you will not find peace in this world, on an individual or a collective level, unless you change the program, the program being guilt. Unless you get back to the mind, unless you make the call to the programmer of your particular software, nothing will change. Unless we get back to the mind and choose a different programmer, one who is sane instead of insane, we will continue to hit A and get E. We will continue to think we are being loving, kind, and compassionate when we are truly being hateful and judgmental.

That is what Jesus means in the manual in another of those horrific passages when he says that it does not seem as if concern for people is attack and hate (M-7.4), anymore than merely asking a question is hateful (T-27.IV). It is hateful because that is our program, but we do not know it. We think we are being honest, inquisitive, kind, compassionately sympathetic, etc. But any time we see another body as separate from ours, as different from ours, we are saying that differentiation is real. This is what the *The Song of Prayer* calls "forgiveness-to-destroy" and "healing-to-separate" (S-2.II; S-3.III). It is the hallmark of the unhealed mind. We think we have something the other person does not have, and while we may indeed have information the other person lacks, information does not heal. The only thing that heals is teaching through example:

> The only meaningful contribution the healer can make is to present an example of one whose direction [meaning decision] has been changed

for him, and who no longer believes in nightmares of any kind (T-9.V.7:4).

That is the healed mind of the healed healer.
Unhealed minds think that what heals is their wisdom,
their hands, how they pray, the particular skill they
have. Wrong. That is what attacks, because it reinforces the very thought system that is the source of the
problem. To repeat, "The only meaningful contribution the healer can make is to present an example of
one whose direction has been changed *for* him and
who no longer believes in nightmares of any kind."

The core of all nightmares, as well as every experience in the phenomenal universe is the belief that the
separation from God is real, and that separation and
differentiation are the reality. This makes me different
from you. If you are sick, I am the expert who can heal
you. On the level of form, that may well be the truth,
and I am not saying you should not avail yourself of
that help. Just don't think it is healing. Don't think for
one minute that it will take you home, that it undoes
guilt, or even more to the point, that it undoes the
belief in guilt. It doesn't.

"Be Healed That You May Heal"

If you truly want to help and make a difference in the world, heal yourself. Recall the famous biblical line "Physician, heal thyself." The *Psychotherapy* pamphlet, the first pamphlet Helen had taken down, ends with that very statement: "Physician, heal thyself." If you really want to help people, which means helping to heal their belief in separation, you must provide the example of one who believes that the separation is not real, which means you must experience within yourself that you are no different from the person you are helping. You are different in form perhaps, but not in content. As the text says: "Be healed that you may heal, and suffer not the laws of sin [separation] to be applied to you" (T-27.VI.8:5).

Recall that I began this class by emphasizing the difference between form and content. The big trap that ensnares us is the belief that form is real and makes a difference. Perhaps the greatest trap of all for students of *A Course in Miracles* is their thinking that *A Course in Miracles* is a book with a blue cover. How could this be? If you believe what the Course says is the truth, how could this be true for a *book*? There is no world here. That means there are no books

37

here. Think about what Jesus is saying to you when he says that eyes do not see and brains do not think, when your eyes have just read something in a book you think is here, and then you think you are thinking about what the book says? He is telling you that this experience is an illusion and therefore not what it seems.

This is a difficult course because it is uncompromising. Its authority is gentle, kind, and loving, but absolute and unequivocal in its teaching. While Helen argued with Jesus all the time, she never argued about what this book said. Never. She argued about the *way* he said it, but she never argued with what it said, because she knew it was the truth. If you believe this book is the truth, you know there is no book, which means you are really studying a thought that is in your mind. The *you* that is studying is not the *you* that you see in your bathroom mirror every morning. The *you* that is studying the Course is a decision-making mind that has recognized that the ego lied, and that there is another teacher in the mind to whom to go. Further, because you think you are a body with a name, you give that teacher a name, too. To repeat this important point, *A Course in Miracles* gives only two choices: the Holy Spirit or Jesus, but they are symbols only.

We are told in the text that "neither sign nor symbol should be confused with source…" (T-19.IV-C.11:2). And so Jesus cautions us: *Do not confuse symbol with source*. The source is love, undifferentiated and non-specific. The symbol is the name we give to that abstract, non-specific thought, just as we give a name to what we think we are. The names themselves (*form*) do not matter, but the thought they represent (*content*) most certainly does.

The non-specific thought that we represent is a thought of separation and guilt, which then becomes embodied in a body, pardon the pun. We then think that is who we are. But we are just a symbol of the mind's decision for a thought, just as the one we call Jesus is a symbol of the mind's decision for a thought of love. Instead of a thought of separation and guilt, the mind can choose the correcting thought of for-giveness, peace, and love. When we choose to iden-tify with the peace and love that is non-specific, but believe we are specific, our mind takes the non-spe-cific thought and translates it into something specific, just as the brain takes the upside-down image that is cast on the retina—if you remember your high school science classes—and translates it into a right-side-up perception that is literally not how we see. Our eyes literally see the world upside down until the brain corrects it, without our even knowing it has been done.

And so, without our knowing it does it, the mind takes our decision for the Atonement, the thought that says the separation never happened, and translates it into something specific. We have so many different names for that. Again, the Course uses only two. Actually, we can say three: Jesus, the Holy Spirit, and *A Course in Miracles.* So while we think that as bodies we are studying *A Course in Miracles*, a book dictated by Jesus through the Holy Spirit to a woman named Helen, we learn that all that is simply a projection of the mind's decision to be right-minded, and the decision to learn that the problem was that we took the *tiny, mad idea* seriously and remembered not to laugh at it (T-27.VIII.6:2-3).

Translated into our everyday experience, this means that whenever we are tempted to get upset, anxious, angry, or guilty—whether it is over something trivial such as the way someone is driving, a terrible event we heard about on the news, or a life-threatening situation that is happening to ourselves, family, or friends—we now have a means of saying "I am never upset for the reason I think" (W-pI.5). We realize that what goes on in the world is a projection of a decision the mind has made for the ego. And when it did so, it also did something else. It said, "I am deciding to be an ego, a separated thought that will culminate in being a separated body. But to avoid the wrath of God, I will take my belief in the sin of separation and split it, keeping the separated state and getting rid of the sin through projection." Every one of us, without exception, has made that decision, and continues to do so. This is what the Course refers to as the ego's secret wish, an image that we want to be true (T-24.VII.8:10).

The image that we want to be true is that we are separated and innocent. We exist as individuals, but are sin-less. Where did the sin go? It went to everyone in the world: to public figures and private people in our lives. Through the "blessings" of projection, the ego tells us, we successfully are freed of sin. Thus, the reason I am upset is not that I pushed Jesus out of the car while I was driving down the freeway; the reason I am upset is that someone cut me off on the freeway. And if no one is on the road, I will still believe someone cut me off, or else there was a pot hole that someone did not fill. All that is a lie! The entire world exists for the purpose of serving the lie. In fact, the world was made so that we could escape God's retributive anger by keeping the separate self we believe we stole from Him, but giving the sin away by projecting

41

it. This is why Jesus told Helen and Bill that the only advantage to their being psychologists was that they understood projection, as I mentioned earlier.

Projection says the problem is not in me; it is in everyone else. The problem is not that my mind chose the wrong teacher or the wrong reaction to the *tiny, mad idea*. The problem is outside me. I am depressed because my loved one died, I lost my job, or I lost four-fifths of my life savings in the stock market. Or, or, or—it is all a lie because if we had chosen to remain with our inner teacher, by whatever name we give it, and we felt its love and peace, nothing that went on outside us could ever affect us. Absolutely nothing. That is both the good and the bad news. It is good news because that is what will truly save us from the horror of our existence. It is bad news because we can no longer blame anyone for anything, including our own bodies.

Since all this is an illusion and a dream, why did we do such an absolutely atrocious job in making the body? One could not ask for a more imperfect instrument to be housed in. It is always in a heightened state of need, needing to breathe, eat, drink, sleep, excrete, recreate, and on and on. Not only is the body needy in a multitude of ways, but it also becomes sick, and as we get older, it fails us more and more and more. Why did we ever do this? It is our dream, our script. Since we could have made so many different homes for our self, why did we make such a vulnerable one? There was a method to our madness, a very good reason for the body being what it is. Our failing, need-driven body is always exclaiming, "I exist, but it is not my fault. It is not my fault that I follow the so-called natural laws that say that I change and deteriorate, my systems will fail and not work all the time, and in the end I will die. And probably before I die, the bodies of my loved ones will die first, leaving me feeling bereft and abandoned."

All of this is what drives Jesus to say, at the beginning of Chapter 13: "If this were the real world, God *would* be cruel" (T-13.in.3:1). He says of this world that it is "the delusional system of those made mad by guilt" (T-13.in.2:2). This is the nature of this great world that we want to save, and that we often think is so wonderful: *a delusional system*. A delusional system is insane or psychotic, the product of the mind's decision to make guilt the reality. This cannot help but drive us all insane because guilt says we sinned, an insane thought because we can never separate from our Source. That is the good news to all except our egos.

4. What It Means to Have a Mind

God is not angry, because God does not know about what never happened. The second and third laws of chaos, which I referred to briefly, reflect our telling God what He should believe (T-23.II.4-8). This is a not-so-subtle reference to the biblical God Who believes what our egos wanted Him to believe: we are sinners. And so our Creator believes it. The whole thing is insane, and the only sane thing we can say about our experiences in this world is that "I am never upset for the reason I think" (W-pI.5). Our mind chose against God, the Holy Spirit, Jesus, and against the thought system of Atonement. *That* is why we are upset. One more time: how can an illusory, hallucinatory world affect us?

When we choose against truth, we believe we attacked it, what the ego calls sin. We are overwhelmed with the guilt over what we have done, believing we will be punished for our sin. Thus we are afraid. If the *decision* for guilt is the problem, what do we do? The ego tells us to get rid of the guilt (projection). That is why we made up a world and fragmented the one self into billions of trillions, and trillions of billions of pieces, providing ourselves with ample opportunities and ample objects onto whom we can project. And project we do, like crazy. And if I do not project onto your body, I project onto mine. It

makes no difference because my body is as much outside my mind as your body is. Bodies do what the
mind tells them to do. They do not get sick, for example, for how can a puppet be sick? It is the mind that
believes in the separation that is sick.

This is such a crucial point in this course. We will
never understand it or successfully apply its principles in our lives if we think it is about us as bodies, as
persons. It is only about the non-personal mind. We
cannot gain access to that mind directly because of
our fear, which is why we all left the mind in the first
place. The ego tells us the mind is a terrible place to
be because if we stay there God will destroy us. There
is a section in the text called "The Fear to Look
Within" that has the ego say to us: Do not look within
because "if you do your eyes will light on sin, and
God will strike you blind" (T-21.IV.2:3), a euphemis-
tic way of saying that if we go within the mind, we
will come face to face with our sin and God will
destroy us.

In the manual, "How Do God's Teachers Deal with
Magic Thoughts?" (M-17) talks about this dynamic.
One line says, "Think not He has forgotten"
(M-17.7:4). Do not for one minute think that God has
forgotten what you did. Imagine the terror that must
strike in us. The universe was made to cover the terror

45

of that thought, which is filled out later in the section: "An angry father pursues his guilty son. Kill or be killed…" (M-17.7:10-11). Once again, the cosmos and all the individual lives within it have one single purpose: to keep these horrifying thoughts buried: "Think not He has forgotten." "An angry father pursues his guilty son. Kill or be killed." A more devastatingly painful thought cannot be imagined, and is the ultimate source of all our nightmares, waking or sleeping.

And so we project our guilt, magically hoping that what we project from the mind is out of our mind. But *ideas leave not their source*. The problem is we do not know we have a source. Forget about God for the moment. We do not know that we have a source in the mind. We do not even know that we have a mind. Because of this, Jesus teaches us how to gain access to the mind indirectly, and says to us: "Whenever you are tempted to be upset about anything in this world, tempted to believe there is anything positive in this world that you want, or need for your salvation and happiness, go to your new Teacher, Whom this course trains you to go to. And simply say Help." The help that Jesus gives is expressed in this one sentence: The world you see is an "outside picture of an inward condition" (T-21.in.1:5). You can skip the rest of the text, and you do not have to do the workbook lessons any-more—you can tell Jesus I said that—as long as you continually keep that one sentence in mind: The world you see is an "outside picture of an inward condition," meaning there is no world out there. The same thought comes in Lesson 23: "Each of your percep-tions of 'external reality' is a pictorial representation of your own attack thoughts" (W-pI.23.3:2). Either sentence would work.

Anything "out here" that we believe has power to affect us, to make us happy or sad, is nothing more or less than a pictorial representation, an outside picture, a projection of the inward condition. The "inner" or "inward" is the mind, and the "condition" is the mind's decision-making ability. "Everything we see outside" does not mean what our eyes see, but how we *react* to what our eyes see. What the eye sees is per-fectly neutral. Anything in the world is neutral. It is what the mind does with it that establishes its value: either the ego's wish to mire us in the dream, never to awaken from it, or the Holy Spirit's goal of helping us awaken from it and returning home. Anything out here that we believe has power over us becomes our means of gaining access to a mind we never knew existed, because the world was made to cover the mind. This is *A Course in Miracles*' great value for us.

4. WHAT IT MEANS TO HAVE A MIND

It is what our inner teacher is continually helping us learn. It is the only right-minded purpose this world serves. It becomes a classroom instead of a prison or playground, a classroom in which we learn the salvific lesson that we are a mind and that forgiveness is truly the key to happiness (W-pI.121).

5. Forgiveness: A Decision of the Mind

Forgiveness is the essence of the Course's message, and we cannot forgive unless we know we are a mind. In *The Song of Prayer*, at the end of the chapter on forgiveness, Jesus tells us not to set forgiveness "in an earthly frame" (S-2.III.7:3). In other words, we are asked not to see forgiveness as something that occurs between bodies or persons. It is a decision made in the mind, by the mind, for the mind's healing. It has nothing to do with bodies. In "The Two Pictures" Jesus says the same thing in different words: we have put the right picture in the wrong frame (T-17.IV.13:1). The right picture is forgiveness; the wrong frame is the body, or in the context of that section, the special relationships between bodies. *A Course in Miracles* is all about our returning to the mind so we may choose again.

At the beginning of the text there is some material that was originally a message for Helen as she was taking down the Course, but obviously it is for everyone. Helen was complaining to Jesus about being afraid and wanting his help. And he said to her:

5. FORGIVENESS: A DECISION OF THE MIND

> The correction of fear *is* your responsibility.
> When you ask for release from fear, you are im-
> plying that it is not (T-2.VI.4:1-2).

Jesus is saying to his scribe, and to all of us: "When
you ask me to take your fear away, something outside
that is making you phobic, anxious, or fearful, you are
saying it is not your responsibility—you did not
choose it":

> You should ask, instead, for help in the condi-
> tions that have brought the fear about. These
> conditions always entail a willingness to be sepa-
> rate. At that level you *can* help it. You are much
> too tolerant of mind wandering, and are pas-
> sively condoning your mind's miscreations
> (T-2.VI.4:3-6).

"Mind wandering" is projection, our wandering from
the mind into the world. This is why Jesus is saying:
"Do not ask me to help you in the world. How can I
help you in a world I know does not exist? I am not
insane. You are. Ask me instead to help you undo the
conditions that brought the fear about." These conditions are the willingness, which refers to our mind's
decision, to be separate, meaning "to be separate
from *me*." Our elder brother and teacher is telling us
that the reason we are afraid is always because we

separated from him and his love. He pleads with us to let him help us undo the cause of our fear.

Since the point was obviously lost, Jesus repeated the lesson shortly afterward:

> You may still complain about fear [his original words to Helen were: you *are* still complaining about fear], but you nevertheless persist in making yourself fearful (T-2.VII.1:1).

The *you* that is making yourself fearful is the mind. Once again, we are told *not* to keep asking Jesus for help in a world he knows is not there and therefore is not the problem.

> I have already indicated that you cannot ask me to release you from fear. I know it does not exist, but you do not. If I intervened between your thoughts and their results, I would be tampering with a basic law of cause and effect; the most fundamental law there is. I would hardly help you if I depreciated the power of your own thinking. This would be in direct opposition to the purpose of this course (T-2.VII.1:2-6).

Clearly what Jesus was telling Helen—and, again, all of us—is that the mind is the cause and the experience of fear is the effect. If we ask him to do something with the effect, with the world of puppets, he would be tampering with the law of cause (mind) and effect (world or body), and therefore would not be helping us. The only way his love can heal is by his teaching us to appreciate the power of our thinking, respecting the power of the mind to choose thoughts of love or fear. Very succinctly, that is the purpose of this course.

This writing occurred in the very early weeks of the scribing, which took a total of seven years. Jesus was making the central message of his course clear to Helen and Bill and to all of us, right at the outset: "If I did what you asked me to do in the world, get you parking spaces, win the lottery for you, heal you of cancer, bring peace to the Middle East, I would be depreciating the power of your mind and serving your ego. This would go against the purpose of this course, which is to return to you the awareness of your mind's power to choose."

The unhealed mind thinks that it can do something in the world. Yet how could we be doing something in an illusory world with a body that does not exist? We can be true healers only when we recognize the problem is our mistaken decision, thinking there is a person out there who needs help. We think there is a world that needs peace brought to it, a planet that is endangered, a species threatened by extinction. What is extinct? Everyone here is extinct. Why do we focus on a certain species when we are not even here? This may sound funny, but that is what *A Course in Miracles* is truly about. It is so easily misunderstood because people think it is about bodies, about a world, about us as persons asking another person named Jesus or the Holy Spirit for help. That makes no sense. This course is only about returning to the mind, appreciating the power of the mind to choose, and to choose differently. This is what heals our minds and makes us healed healers. The process involves using the forms of the world as a way of gaining access to the content of the mind's mistaken decision so we may choose again. Finally, remember that the Course is aimed at the mind's decision maker, that we may remember that it is our identity within the dream.

Before proceeding with questions, I would like to read a passage from the teachers' manual. It is a lovely expression of what it means to be a healed mind. It is in the section called "How Is Healing Accomplished?" (M-5). The third part of the answer to that question is discussed under the heading of "The Function of the Teacher of God" (M-5.III). Its specific focus is on what we do when we are in the presence of those who believe they are sick. We begin with the second paragraph:

(M-5.III.2:1) To them God's teachers come, to represent another choice which they had forgotten.

We all find ourselves in a situation of pain, distress, or discomfort, and have forgotten there is another choice we can make. The ego, as we have seen, has very effectively removed that choice from our awareness by making us mindless.

(M-5.III.2:2) The simple presence of a teacher of God is a reminder.

Let's say that you are sick and I come to you in my right mind. The sickness is your proof that you are separate from God, and that your sin and guilt deserve punishment, sickness being part of the punishment. On another level, the sickness is something you have chosen as payment back to God for what you took from Him. When I am with you and in my right mind, feeling Jesus' love with me, I know that the separation is illusory. That certainty is with me all the while I am with you in your pain. We are not speaking of what I do or say on the bodily level, but only about the thoughts in my mind: peace, love, and my not making your error real by letting your pain and sickness disrupt my peace. In other words, deep within me I am not guilty about your sickness, nor am I worried about it. The love and the peace of God is with me despite what seems to be happening to you. What I am then saying to you, because minds are joined, is that you do not have to be upset, God is not angry. The source of your pain is the belief that God does not love you, because you do not love Him. The peace and love I am demonstrating, regardless of their form, is saying to you that just as I am not separate from you, God is not separate from you. This means that my peaceful and defenseless presence is healing because it reminds you that your decision-making mind can choose again.

(M-5.III.2:3) His thoughts ask for the right to question what the patient has accepted as true.

If you are sick, it means that you have accepted as true that the error of separation is real and beyond question. You made the choice to identify with the ego that tells you that you are sinful, guilty, fearful, and that your suffering and pain is what you deserve because of what you have done. The error, your sin against God, is real and cannot be questioned because you do not even know there is a question. Your sickness is a fact. Once we accept something as true, we never again question it.

My being with you as a healed mind is asking you to question what you never believed you could question. I am telling you there is another way of being in this world, a way that is peaceful and does not make the error real. Because I have accepted the Love of God in my mind, you must have, too, since minds are joined, even if you are not aware of having done so. If I am identified with that Love and demonstrate it to you, I cannot be separate from it. And since you and I are not separate, if I am not separate from God's Love, then you are not. My very presence is saying to you: "Question the validity of the judgment you have made that you are separated. Sin is not real, the error is not real, and these thoughts are all made up."

(M-5.III.2:4) As God's messengers, His teachers are the symbols of salvation.

If salvation for us is the Presence of the Holy Spirit in our mind, the home of the Atonement principle, I become a symbol of its love when I accept its truth. Jesus says that he is the manifestation of the Holy Spirit (C-6.1:1), and the Course also says that he is asking us to become his manifestation (C-6.5:1-4). Since Jesus is no longer in the body, one of the purposes of *A Course in Miracles* is to help us become his manifestation.

(M-5.III.2:5-6) They ask the patient for forgiveness for God's Son in his own Name. They stand for the Alternative.

By saying the error is not real, we are saying there is nothing that has to be forgiven, the ultimate meaning of forgiveness. The healed healer then stands for the Alternative. The upper case *A* signifies that we now represent the Holy Spirit, and as healed minds we become His manifestation to others in the dream.

(M-5.III.2:7) With God's Word in their mind they come in benediction, not to heal the sick but to remind them of the remedy God has already given them.

Note that the phrase "Word of God" almost always refers to some aspect of the Atonement principle.

This is an extremely important statement. We come not to solve problems or heal the sick, because that is what unhealed healers do. Their unhealed minds make the error real in the world and the body, setting the stage for them to fix it: solving the external problem and healing the sick body. But there is no world to fix or body to be healed. Thus God's teachers come "not to heal the sick but to remind them of the remedy God has already given them." The Holy Spirit is simply the reminder to the decision-making mind that it can choose differently.

This is why when we are right-minded, living in this world is easy. We do not do anything. Jesus had the easiest job of anyone. He did not do anything. He did not have to do anything, he simply was. The Course says, "We say 'God is,' and then we cease to speak, for in that knowledge words are meaningless" (W-pI.169.5:4). Forget the gospel stories, Jesus did not heal anyone. The Love of the Holy Spirit *in his mind* healed through him. He did not do anything. You do not have to do anything. This does not mean that our body does not function. Obviously, Jesus' body did a lot, and our bodies do a lot. Rather, we realize that we are not the agent of what the body does, but of the love that comes through us. And so we need do nothing. It made no difference to Jesus, if for the moment we follow the biblical narrative, whether he was crucified on his last day on earth, or took a leisurely walk in the garden. It made no difference because he knew he was not his body. Love flowed through him, and whatever love did made no difference to him. He knew that love is in the mind, not the body.

That is what teachers of God do—*nothing*. They simply come and represent the Alternative. Again, this does not mean they do not say things, or bring flowers or candy to a hospital room, or take a friend to the doctor. They may do all those things (or none of them), as we had discussed earlier, but they realize that they are not the ones who do them. Consequently, there are no feelings of imposition, fatigue, exhaustion, or resentment; there is no misplaced pity. There is nothing except the realization that they are the instruments of God's Love coming through their minds, expressed in their bodies.

(M-5.III.2:8-10) It is not their hands that heal. It is not their voice that speaks the Word of God. They merely give what has been given them.

One more time, this does not mean we do not lay hands on people if that is what we feel will help, or that the sick feel will help. It does not mean we do not read a line from the Course or the Bible, or from any other book if that is what would be helpful. It is fine to do any of these things as long as on some level we know that it does not heal, because it is of the body and that makes the error real. What alone heals is the love in our minds, which comes through our bodies in whatever form is kind and loving.

Again, to make this very clear, we are not *not* to do things with our bodies. It is simply that we do not become confused that it is *our* hands, *our* words, *our* meditation, or anything else that does it. In truth, nothing has to be done because there is no problem—the separation never happened. This is the crucial point. Unhealed healers believe something has to be done and they know how to do it. Their unhealed minds have made the error of separation real, leading them to believe that they are God. But healed healers simply accept the healing within, allowing the love in their minds to extend through them: "They merely give what has been given them."

(M-5.III.2:11-12) Very gently they call to their brothers to turn away from death: "Behold, you Son of God, what life can offer you. Would you choose sickness in place of this?"

The first sentence does not mean that you necessarily call someone away literally, but the love in your mind says, to paraphrase the famous lines of Moses, "Choose life, not death." This love does that of itself, saying: "Behold, you Son of God, 'would you choose sickness in place of this?'" It is our right mind's love that is freed to call out to others and serve as a reminder. That is all the Holy Spirit does, it is what the person we call Jesus did, and it is what he is helping us do as healed minds.

Part Two

6. Discussion

Asking Jesus for Help

Q: I have a question regarding asking Jesus for help. You think that we should not ask for help with things in the world. What I do not understand is the kind of help I am receiving by asking Jesus, because you also say there is nothing real here.

A: I'll tell you a story that I've told many times. Helen once asked Jesus what she should say to someone who was in trouble. Now we would all think that was a perfectly right-minded thing to do. This was his response, which came in a message that she wrote down: "Don't ask me what you should say to this brother. Ask me instead for help that you look at him through the eyes of peace and not judgment." This is a wonderful way of encapsulating what it means to ask for help. Jesus was telling Helen not to ask him what she should do or say, but to ask instead for help to look through the eyes of peace and not judgment. In other words, we ask our older brother for help to correct our misperceptions. Rather than seeing someone or some situation as external and capable of affecting us, we ask for help to see it as simply irrelevant to our peace of mind. I am not talking about not caring what goes on. I am talking about not giving power to what goes on around us to affect us. It is not that we not do things in the world—as bodies we all have to do things in the world—we just want to be sure that what we do comes from what the Course calls "the quiet center" (T-18.VII.8).

A wonderful way of talking about what the miracle does comes at the beginning of Chapter 28:

> The miracle does nothing. All it does is to undo. And thus it cancels out the interference to what has been done. It does not add, but merely takes away (T-28.I.1:1-4).

This is saying that we ask for help in canceling out the interference, undoing whatever special investment we have in the outcome, whether it be in a relationship, world situation, or something involving our body. We ask for help to be at peace regardless of what is going on. At that point, anything we do would be helpful. Jesus ended the message to Helen that I just quoted by saying that "all the angels in Heaven will then come to your aid," meaning that when there is no guilt or specialness in our minds, the love that is there will simply flow out, *and we will know exactly what to do and what to say.* This is what is really important. It is what Jesus meant in *The Song of Prayer* when he said that it is the song we want, not its parts: the echoes, harmonics, or intervals. We want the song itself. We want the love (*content*), not a little fragment (*form*) of the love (see S-1.I).

Whether we associate that love with Jesus or any other symbol does not matter. We want some experience of that love and peace that embraces everyone. From that experience, we will automatically know what to do and say. We need not ask anymore because we have already gotten the interference out of the way, allowing the love to extend through us, informing our words and actions so that they can only be kind and loving.

We do not even worry about the mind or where it is. Lesson 5 suffices: "I am never upset for the reason I think" (W-pI.5). The core of the process of forgiveness, or healing, is withdrawing our projections, as we saw in Part One. That is all we need do. In effect, the miracle takes our attention away from the world and directs it to the mind. As long as our attention is no longer on something outside, even if we do not know there is an inside, we are automatically back in the mind. This book is called *A Course in Miracles* because *the miracle* is the term for the reversal of projection, which it undoes and sets the stage for the change of mind that *is* the healer.

Are We God?

Q: This is about God being spirit and perfect Oneness. Are we that also? Are we that Oneness, and wouldn't that make us God? Somehow that doesn't seem right.

A: Yes, that is true, but let me talk about it, because if you take it out of context it does sound silly, if not arrogant. The "we" that is perfectly whole and perfectly one is not the "we" we think we are. It is the "we" that is the collective Son, or Christ, that is perfectly at one with its Creator, "a Oneness joined as One" (T-25.I.7:1). That is Who We are, and since there is nothing outside God, in that sense we are God. But it is not "we" as a person. This has nothing to do with anything of the body or individuality, but only the mind that, when it is healed, remembers that it is in truth a Mind.

This wholeness is not like a pie or a jigsaw puzzle with all the pieces together. What defines God's Son is wholeness. Early in the text, Jesus in effect says that the whole of Christ is greater than the sum of its parts (T-2.VII.6:1-3).This is not what we studied in high school geometry, where we learned that the whole is equal to the sum of its parts. The whole *is* greater than the sum of its parts because Christ, our true Self, is perfectly indivisible and whole. That wholeness defines the Sonship. It is not that we are all these separate pieces that have come together. We were never separated! We are the wholeness of Christ, and since there is no Trinity, no Father, Son, and Holy Spirit, in that sense, and that sense only, we are all God.

Changing One's Mind versus Changing the Form

Q: The workbook says if we are in our right minds, God's Will is our will.

A: Yes, of course, because there is only one Will.

Q: So is that how a change of thinking can help?

A: Yes, that is how a change of thinking changes everything. It does not necessarily change the forms, but when you are truly right-minded, you are not involved with the form. That does not mean that your body is not involved in the form, but it does mean that you know you are not your body. There are a number of passages that say the same thing with a different subject (e.g., T-16.II.1-2): our responsibility is to *choose* forgiveness or the miracle; their *extension* through us is not our responsibility. Our job is only to get the ego out of the way, for then anything we do or say will be loving because there will be nothing else in our minds.

If I am in my right mind, I am not in my wrong mind, because it is one or the other. Think of a car in which there are only two gears: drive and reverse—no low, second, third, or overdrive. We have drive and reverse, and we cannot do both at the same time. When I am in my right mind there is no ego, and therefore anything I say is coming from the Holy Spirit. As we approach the end of the journey, we realize we *are* the Holy Spirit.

We personify the Holy Spirit and Jesus because we still think we are bodies. Another line I frequently cite says, "You cannot even think of God without a body, or in some form you think you recognize" (T-18.VIII.1:7). Because that is true, the Course talks about God as a body and as a person. He is even called Father. He is so anthropomorphized that He has arms, hands, a voice, eyes, and tear ducts (because He weeps). All these are metaphors. There is one passage that explains this: "Since you believe that you are separate, Heaven presents itself to you as separate…"

(T-25.I.5:1). But the fact of the matter is that God is not a body. Jesus is not a body. The Holy Spirit is not a body. *A Course in Miracles* is about the Holy Spirit being our Teacher; yet the very end of it describes Him as an illusion that will disappear as form (C-6.1:4-5; 5:8). The *Thought* of perfect love, however, will not disappear, for that is Who we are.

Again, as we near the end of the journey, we realize we *are* the Holy Spirit, we *are* the voice of Jesus because there is no other voice. To the extent that I no longer identify as a person or body, but more and more as a mind, more and more as a right mind, I realize that I *am* the Voice for God. At the very end, we become God, in the sense of disappearing into His Heart (W-pII.14.5:5). This is when the dream dissolves and we no longer experience anything because there is nothing in us to experience, and nothing there to even experience the nothing. This is a level so far beyond us at this stage of our journey that there is no point in engaging in what the Course calls "senseless musings." It is senseless to speak about what we cannot begin to understand.

Unfortunately, when we use those words, "I am God," it is so easy to think of the "I" as the self we think we are, as I just commented on. This is not what

6. DISCUSSION

we are talking about and certainly not what the Course is talking about. It teaches us that as part of perfect Love, we *are* that Love, but this is meaningless to us and subject to distortion as long as we think we are separated. And we clearly do, for when we awaken every morning and look in the mirror, we see a self we believe is real, that has a name that people call and we respond to. Thinking that is who we are means, again, that to speak of a "Oneness joined as One" or being part of perfect Love makes no sense. At one point, when Jesus is discussing some of these ideas that we cannot understand, he suddenly stops and says we cannot understand what he is speaking about, so let us return to what we can understand, which is learning to forgive (W-pI.169.9-11).

Forgiveness is recalling the projections. To say that another way, if what we are projecting is the thought of separation, then when we project it out it takes the form of the belief in separate interests; my interests are separate from yours. For instance, let us say both of us are vying for the same job. We both cannot have it, so our interests are separate. You want the job for yourself. I want the job for myself. If you make the body real and therefore your experiences here real, the *one or the other* principle becomes very important. It is only when you realize that you are a mind and not a body that you understand that no one loses and everyone wins. Surely, on the level of form one person will get the job and another person will not, but what are we talking about? What job? What body? Jesus is asking us to act in the world of symbols, but not because we believe the symbols are the reality. That is, again, what it means to be a healed healer.

An unhealed healer thinks there are separate interests. You have a problem, I do not have that problem, and so I can help you with that problem. That is true on the level of form, but on the level of the mind we both have the same problem because we both think we are here, we both think we are separated, and we both think we need each other for something. I need your money, otherwise I cannot survive. I need your praise and appreciation and you need my expertise to feel better. These kinds of situations are inevitable on the level of the body or form, but the idea is not to take any of it seriously and to recognize that any situation you are in that has the form of being helpful—either you are being helped or you are helping others—is simply an excuse to learn the lesson that we are not different but the same. That recognition is what heals our minds.

The recognition that we are the same, not on the bodily level but on the level of the mind, is another very important theme in *A Course in Miracles*. You have an insane ego; I have an insane ego. You have a sane correction (the Holy Spirit); I have a sane correction. And we both have the same power to choose between them. Where, then, is the difference? Your form is this, my form is that; yet they are alike because forms are illusory.

Another very important line is "Nothing so blinding as perception of form" (T-22.III.6:7). Form lies. As I am teaching, I look out at a sea of separate bodies in separate chairs, with wall-hangings in the background, and so on. It is all a lie, projections of a delusional thought system. When you project a delusional thought, you hallucinate. The Course uses this word deliberately (T-20.VIII.7-8), as it does with other psychiatric terminology. One who hallucinates sees what is not there, hears voices that are not present, etc. These are symptoms of psychosis, which is why we are told over and over that we are insane.

The choice of this language is not a put-down of us, but simply a statement that says: "Look, you have to see what is going on. And what is going on is not 'out there'; it is in your mind." The unhealed healer thinks there is something "out there" that needs healing. Thinking like that makes the error real. Believing there is an external problem that needs resolution means that you will never be healed, for you will be teaching the ego's thought system. You may disguise it behind thoughts that you are helpful, kind, and compassionate, but all you are really doing is saying "I, I, I, I," the first person pronoun that is sacred to the ego and the unhealed mind.

When we are right-minded, we will use the same situation of helping or being helped as a means of learning that, on the level of mind, we are all the same. We need to be faithful to the form, our roles and responsibilities as individuals, family members, employees, etc. We are faithful to these various roles not because they are meaningful in and of themselves, but because they are the classrooms we have chosen in which we learn we are not guilty, that everyone involved in the situation has the same interest of awakening from this insane dream. Because we think we are bodies, we need these classrooms of learning until we learn we are not bodies.

To reiterate this important point, we are not asked to deny what goes on in the world, or our various responsibilities. The Course would actually say just the opposite. We want to learn to fulfill our responsibilities and roles without guilt, resentment, fear, or anger. As our minds are increasingly healed, we will be freer and freer to deal with every situation with kindness, not just to certain people on certain days in certain situations, but to everyone all the time. When we come from the loving presence of Jesus in our mind, how could we not embrace everyone the way he does? We would no longer choose up sides or differentiate good and evil, victim and victimizer, oppressed and oppressor. We would see everyone as the same because everyone *is* the same.

The closest we come in this world to Heaven's Oneness is the perception that everyone is the same. That is the meaning of the New Year's resolution that comes at the end of Chapter 15, which was actually written at New Year's: "Make this year different by making it all the same" (T-15.XI.10:11). Make this year different from all the other years by seeing everyone, every situation, every relationship as the same, not in form but in content. Form lies. Perception of differences is a lie. Do not believe anyone who comes from a perception of differences. I always like to remind people that Jesus flunked high school arithmetic because he could not add past one. The only number he knows is one, because everyone is part of the one. We are all the same.

This is the point at which we can see the practicality of *A Course in Miracles*, for with our healed perception we would go through our days recognizing how tempted we are to make differences real. When we are in that state of peace, it would not matter what goes on around us; we would still be peaceful. On the level of behavior and form, we would act differently, of course. We would treat people differently because it would not be appropriate to act the same way toward everyone. But the loving *content* would not change. The purpose is always to have our help, kindness, and true compassion embrace all living things. That is the Buddha's great teaching: compassion for *all* living things.

If you re-read the Course from beginning to end, you will be astonished at how often the words *all, every, everyone,* and *everything* occur, not to mention the concept of all-inclusiveness. Forgiveness is for *all* or it is for none. You forgive *everyone* or you forgive no one. At the end of the text, in Jesus' beautiful final vision, he says, "Yet this a vision is which you must share with everyone you see, for otherwise you will behold it not" (T-31.VIII.8:5). The vision is that we are all part of God's one Son. *This a vision is which you must share with everyone you see, for otherwise you will behold it not* because the vision is all-inclusive. An earlier line says, "Vision or judgment is your choice, but never both of these" (T-20.V.4:7). It is one or the other. Judgment always distinguishes and differentiates, saying there is good and bad, innocent and guilty. Vision sees everyone as the same, reflecting Heaven's truth of perfect Oneness. This is what distinguishes the unhealed from the healed mind, which knows that all minds are the same, sharing a common need and purpose.

The Extremes of Guilt

Q: Increasingly, it seems like every time I have to make a decision about anything it is torture. It could be the most mundane thing in the world, like where to get gas. And if I choose to get gas in one place, I will feel guilty for not getting it in another place, which makes me wrong. Every moment is pressure, and I know that when the breakthroughs happen, they are gone. Yet they come back. It is as if there were a jury up here, and it is non-stop. I see the projections. I see when I walk around the house things seem fine. Then one person says the wrong thing and I am upset, even though I understand that they didn't do anything. I feel guilty for being upset, and yet it doesn't seem as if I can ever have a life outside this horrible guilt.

A: I am not going to say anything you do not know. What you want to do, which I think you are already doing, is realize the absurdity of your situation. Your feelings of guilt are really what I described earlier: you are taking the *tiny, mad idea* seriously, to such an extreme that you feel guilty about the gas station or anything you obsess about, something you know is ludicrous. That is helpful because it points out the utter absurdity of the position of taking something inherently meaningless and making it into something serious and guilt inducing. All you want to do is be aware of it and not take yourself so seriously, even when you already are being very serious.

It feels like a wall that you cannot get through, but you can begin to if you realize it is not what it seems. The ego always loves to make up these walls of problems, neuroses, and the like, and then come up with ingenious ways of breaking the wall down, going around it, or avoiding it entirely. Yet all you have to do is look at the wall and realize its inherent nothingness. This is the gentle laughter the Course talks about. You laugh at yourself for being so serious about nothing. And *everything* is nothing, whether you are talking about a gas station, your kids, wife, or self. They are the same. In other words, don't allow yourself to be fooled by the ego's seriousness.

Critical Mass / The Hundredth Monkey

Q: The following passage from "The Last Judgment" in Chapter 2 is sometimes interpreted as "critical mass" or the "hundredth monkey" idea. We all stay here until everyone else goes:

> ...God has only *one* Son.... every one must be an integral part.... However, this is obscured as long as any of its parts is missing. That is why the conflict cannot ultimately be resolved until all the parts of the Sonship have returned. Only then can the meaning of wholeness in the true sense be understood (T-2.VII.6:1-2, 4-6).

A: If that passage and others like it are taken out of context, it certainly sounds like the critical mass idea. It is important to remember, however, that the early chapters are not as clear as the later ones, and this passage is from Chapter 2. These early chapters also occasionally talk about miracles as something we do, something we "perform," while the rest of the Course makes very clear that miracles have nothing to do with bodies. Miracles are not something we perform;

they are something we *undo* in our mind. Recall: "The miracle does nothing. All it does is to undo" (T-28.I.1:1-2).

If we were to take everything we read in *A Course in Miracles* as literally true, then someone like Jesus who has transcended his ego and is in the real world would have to wait for every single person to change his or her mind before returning home to God. That way of thinking is contradicted in the teachers' manual in a discussion of the question, "How Many Teachers of God Are Needed to Save the World?" (M-12). The answer given is "one"—and that one is not necessarily Jesus. It could be, but it could be anyone, because when your individual mind is healed, you realize there is no individual mind, no separation, no separate parts to the Sonship. The workbook teaches, "When I am healed I am not healed alone" (W-pI.137). The healed mind realizes we are all one mind, and the one mind never left its source. That recognition is the end of the ego and its world.

Thus, this passage from Chapter 2 of the text must be understood as reflecting the world's point of view. Another passage in the text states that "just as the separation occurred over millions of years, the Last Judgment will extend over a similarly long period..."

6. DISCUSSION

(T-2.VIII.2:5). This implies that linear time is real. In contrast, the passage quoted above from the manual, and practically everything else in the Course, is from the point of view of the healed mind. We need to remember that large parts of the early chapters were written as a dialogue between Helen and Jesus, and that the writing was heavily influenced, in form not content, by Helen's anxiety and considerable discomfort with the process of scribing. These aspects cleared up by what is now Chapter 5, after which the writing becomes much more fluent, with far fewer inconsistencies in forms of expression.

Since there is no way of understanding the concept of only one teacher of God being needed for the world's salvation, the above passage from Chapter 2 is for those of us stuck in the dream. The purpose of the discussion of the Last Judgment and the Second Coming, which also occurs there, is to correct the traditional Christian understanding of these terms that are so fraught with fear and guilt. The traditional meaning has Jesus coming back on clouds of glory to judge the good and the bad, the sheep and the goats (Matthew 25:31-46). And woe be unto you if you are a goat! That is serious stuff indeed if you are a Christian. It is a terrifying thought to be on the wrong side, being born on the wrong farm, as it were.

In sum, in those passages Jesus is using symbols that are associated with intense guilt and fear. He turns them around to make them benevolent and kind. This is why we should not take those passages literally.

Awakening As One

Q: Did it really just happen that when Jesus became enlightened we all became enlightened, but because of the illusory setup of time we do not know it yet? Would that be one way of saying it?

A: It is not so much that when he became enlightened he dragged us all with him, implying we did not want to go. It is rather that when he became enlightened he knew there was no separation, and therefore we were with him when he arose (C-6.5:5; see also M-23.6:8-10). This has nothing to do with the biblical stories. When Jesus awoke from the dream we were with him because we are always with him—we are one. And so it is not that he took us with him. He simply showed that we are already there. In other words, by one person showing that there is no ego, the ego is disproved. This means that everyone's existence, predicated on the ego thought system of separation, is shown to be inherently unreal.

Again, we cannot understand what this course is teaching from the world's point of view, but only when we read it as a mind. If the Course is read from the perspective of the body, it will inevitably be misconstrued and its teachings distorted. And to add insult to injury, a healed mind would not even ask the question.

Doing the Outrageous Thing

Q: In the context of not doing anything out of guilt, can you say something about the passage that says that if your brother asks you for something outrageous, you should do it?

A: Some 100 pages later Jesus returns to that passage; forgetting he used the word *outrageous* and now uses the word *foolish*:

> I have said that if a brother asks a foolish thing of you to do it [T-12.III.4:1]. But be certain that this does not mean to do a foolish thing that would hurt either him or you... (T-16.I.6:4-5).

Jesus did not mean that you should do something out of guilt, because that is harmful to you and harmful to the other person. The idea is that when someone asks you something outrageous and you experience yourself in quick opposition ("I am not going to do such a silly thing!"), you need to realize that this quick opposition comes from the ego. The right mind does not oppose anything. It may not do everything people ask, but it does not oppose. Saying "no" would always be kind and gentle, even if its form is firmness. Quick opposition is never gentle. Thus, when you find yourself quickly opposing something, "I am not going to do that!" the first thing to do is go within, recognizing that the world of outrageous requests you see is an "outside picture of an inward condition." Your mind has chosen to see itself as separate from someone and you are now accentuating that separateness by saying, "I won't do it!" This will inevitably bring guilt because you are making separation real all over again. Before you respond to the other person, you first want to change your wrong-minded response. Once the ego is out of the way, you will do or not do what the person asks, but you will be loving.

A common confusion among students is to think of gentleness as wishy-washy, or firmness as an attack. When we are right-minded, we are firm about doing or not doing something because it is the *kind* thing to do. This is similar to a parent being firm with a child because the child is about to do something that will be harmful to itself. You can be gentle, loving, and still firm as you say, "No. I am sorry, but you cannot do this." Or you could be firm and have the seeming strength of raising your voice and exclaiming: "Grrr, no you cannot do this, and if you do it I will punish you." Jesus models gentle firmness in his course when he does not go along with our illusions: "I will love you and honor you and maintain complete respect for what you have made, but I will not uphold it unless it is true" (T-4.III.7:7). The clarity of his teaching is always kind and respectful.

Then, too, one does not have to let go of limits in order to be gentle, another common misconception. You only let go of the limitations of the ego that say you and I are separate. If you set limits and are firm, but are not being gentle, you are saying differentiation is real: there are good things to do and bad things to do; I am the authority and I am telling you that you cannot do the bad thing. But there is no love in that, no shared interest. Instead, you are simply being authoritarian in forbidding the person from perform- ing certain behavior. We cannot be authoritarian and gentle, but we can, as is Jesus, be gentle, loving, and authoritative.

What attracts people to this course, even if they do not know what it really says, is that it has a clear sense of authority about it, gentle and kind. Jesus is quite clear about saying what the truth is. Like God, Jesus looks at our illusions and simply thinks otherwise (T-23.I.2:7). He does not threateningly shake an accusing finger at us, but merely says: "As long as you are afraid I will wait. I will not drag you to Heaven. I will invite you and help you undo your blocks of fear." As the Gershwin song says, "Who could ask for anything more?"

Trying to drag oneself or others into Heaven is hardly loving. When we attempt this, we are clearly saying that we are *not* in Heaven. Jesus, on the other hand, does not really take us anywhere because we are already there. *He simply reminds us.* There is a passage in Chapter 5, the first place where the Holy Spirit is talked about at any length, in which Jesus says that the Holy Spirit "does not command" or "overcome"; He "merely reminds" (T-5.II.7:1-4). That is what this course does. It reminds us of the truth that we are already home: "You are at home in God, dreaming of exile but perfectly capable of awakening to reality (T-10.I.2:1).

Our awareness has to shift from being an ego and the "home of evil, darkness and sin," to being aware that "light and joy and peace abide in me" (W-pI.93), and that we are already home. What is needed for us to awaken and realize we are already home is to look at our nightmares with Jesus' loving presence beside us, teaching that our fear is not what we thought it was. If the process is not gentle we will not learn the gentleness of love, and we will instead learn what the ego has always told us: God's Love reprimands, scolds, and punishes.

Our goal, therefore, is to be an example of a gentle, kind authority. The key thing is to *want* to be this example. We cannot teach the Course's kind and loving message of forgiveness if we are not ourselves kind, loving, and forgiving. Otherwise we but teach the form and not the content. This makes them discrepant and us conflicted, because the content is guilt and fear while the form appears loving and kind.

A brief passage from the text highlights this inevitable experience of conflict, even if it is unconscious, when form and content are discrepant:

> You may then control your reactions behaviorally, but not emotionally. This would obviously be a split or an attack on the integrity of your mind, pitting one level within it against another (T-12.I.2:4-5).

This is something we all do, and we have taught the world to train us this way. We have the insane belief that by controlling what we do and say, we will be changing what we think—a clear inversion of *cause* and *effect*, *form* and *content*—wherein we believe the problem is bad actions, things we do or say that are not loving. We may believe, for example, that a good student of *A Course in Miracles* does not get angry, and is loving and peaceful all the time. And so, since we aspire to being good Course students, we must never get angry. We attempt to control our behavior, magically hoping that this will do the trick. Yet this accomplishes nothing. The anger remains in the mind, along with the guilt. Even worse, we have the illusion of having solved the problem since our bodily actions (*form*) suggest that our mind is healed (*content*).

It is far better if we are angry that we be angry. Then we can deal with our unhealed mind, rather than pretending that by controlling our behavior (*effect/form*) we are controlling our thoughts (*cause/content*). This is all very tempting because if we control our behavior, people will like us. This is not saying, of course, that every time we have an angry thought, we should act on it. Discipline, as Jesus once told Helen, is very often helpful. But it is essential that we be aware that controlling our behavior does not take care of the problem. Again, the issue in all of this is not to conceal the mind's mistaken decision with "correct" behavior. This is most definitely *not* what Jesus means by demonstration, which is always to lovingly reflect the mind's right-minded choice.

A statement at the beginning of the manual says, "To teach is to demonstrate" (M-in.2:1). It is not the words or form that teaches, but the content. We want to teach by providing an example of someone whose mind has already been changed, a healed healer. Accordingly, Jesus says in "The Unhealed Healer": "A therapist does not heal; *he lets healing be*" (T-9.V.8:1). When we feel that we have to heal or correct someone, we are saying there is a problem out there that needs healing, a person who needs correcting. We are seeing differentiation and separate interests. True therapists *let healing be* by undoing the blocks to their own healing.

What has to be healed is the belief in separate interests. When that belief is undone, its place is automatically taken by the perception of shared interests, and everything we say will come from that. While we may be different in form, we do not see ourselves as different from others because we know that form does not mean anything. Brains and bodies may be different, but minds remain the same.

We are all healers because we are all teachers and students. This has nothing to do with a specific activity that the world calls healing. We simply *let healing be*, and learning to do that is how we are healed. After all, "You need no healing to be healed" (T-28.I.10:8). The process of healing our minds consists of asking for help to choose to undo the ego: our belief in anger, guilt, anxiety, depression, loss, triumph; the belief that using other people to satisfy our own needs is good. That is what we need help with, and as we release our investment in that misperception, the love that is in our and everyone's right mind automatically extends through us. It is essential that the extension of that love not be our concern. What other people do with our words or behavior is irrelevant to the healed mind. We have done our part by getting the ego out of the way. "A therapist does not heal; *he lets healing be*." If you think you are doing something helpful, you are an unhealed healer. *What could be helpful in a world that does not exist?* We must keep coming back to that: *What could be helpful in a world that does not exist?* To think you are doing something helpful is not helpful. That is not healing. That is sharing in a delusion and reinforcing it. It is really saying to another, "Yes, the hallucination is real; you have a problem that I can help you with." Although on the level of form and behavior we may seem to do just that, we are not taken in by the ego's lies, for we know that healing occurs only on the level of the mind. As Lesson 184 states:

> It would indeed be strange if you were asked to go beyond all symbols of the world, forgetting them forever; yet were asked to take a teaching function. You have need to use the symbols of the world a while. But be you not deceived by them as well. They do not stand for anything at all, and in your practicing it is this thought that will release you from them. They become but means by which you can communicate in ways the world can understand, but which you recognize is not the unity where true communication can be found (W-pI.184.9).

Fulfilling Roles While Believing Nothing Is Outside Us

Q: But what trumps everything, and you just said it a few minutes ago, is that there *literally* is no world. I can't keep my mind off that, not that I want to be in denial, not brush my teeth, etc.

A: That is very helpful. We should always hold that awareness somewhere in our minds, for we are kept on the straight and narrow by never forgetting that there is no world out there. This means that anything we are feeling in relationship to the world must be a projection. It is the same as when we dream at night, nothing is really happening in the bedroom. Lots of things are going on while we are asleep, but in reality nothing is happening. It is all a projection, coming from our mind or brain in images we call dreams. But this entire world is a dream. Remember, *perception is interpretation*. Perception is not what our eyes see, but is based on the teacher—the ego or the Holy Spirit—through whose eyes we see. Therefore, everything we experience in the world around us is coming from within. It has to be that way because there is nothing outside us: *ideas leave not their source*. This is why that idea trumps everything. It is what keeps us clear that the problem is never in the world, but in the mind that made the world.

Q: In my profession of computers, in the world of illusion where everybody is very serious about their problems, I go into a serious situation and tend to walk in whistling that everything is okay because it is all an illusion. I still do my job and fix the problem, but underneath I know that it is not about that.

A: That's right, and if you really know that, you won't get anxious, angry, or frustrated; you won't get elated when you solve the problem. You will be even and calm throughout. This will be how you know that you are not mouthing the words that the world is an illusion. Knowing this enables you to be with anyone, do anything, be in any part of the world, and still be peaceful. It does not matter because everything is the same. You have honored that New Year's resolution, "Make this year different by making it all the same…" (T-15.XI.10:11), because you know the problem is not "out there" but "in here" (the mind).

Whatever knowledge and expertise you have that helps you solve problems, whether as a therapist or computer whiz, becomes an excuse for you to teach what you are learning and reinforce its truth in yourself. That is the true meaning of helping others. The teaching comes by being peaceful and defenseless. And the minute you find yourself becoming frustrated or angry, you know you have made the world real again—*the* mistake. When you catch yourself in that ego trap, simply smile at yourself and say, "Oops, I did it again." That's all.

Moreover, you will probably find that you actually get better at your job as a computer programmer. What makes you an ineffective programmer is your anxiety, self-hatred, hatred of others, resentment of what you are being asked to do, and whatever other ego thoughts you have. By getting the ego thoughts out of the way, you have made room for love to come through you and make you a fine programmer, therapist, housewife, parent, child, bricklayer, etc. Regardless of the disparate forms of our many roles, love is the constant content.

Right-minded Healing

False versus True Empathy

Q: How does one right-mindedly see someone who appears to be in a pretty bad situation, like returning from the war with post-traumatic stress disorder? I see their pain, know that their minds are choosing fear that manifests as symptoms, but at the same time the Course teaches that on another level all that is part of our self. I get confused with these different levels.

A: As a neuro-psychologist you deal with people with traumatic symptoms, vets returning from Iraq with brain injuries and the like. Certainly, if you are a professional with expertise in a certain area, you respond in a way appropriate to your role. On one level, you use your training and experience to make an evaluation about the extent of the injury, the prognosis, and a useful course of treatment, including working with the family. This is no different from a plumber making an assessment about a plumbing problem in a home or a business, and then proceeding to correct it.

On another level, at the same time that you proceed professionally, you use the situation as a way of monitoring your own thoughts. You watch yourself becoming horrified by the situation; perhaps a particular symptom is abhorrent to you, or you become impatient with the person, angry at the system that does not allow proper care or treatment, or even angry at the President who declared war and thus is ultimately responsible for these terrible effects. Whatever your ego reactions, this is what you pay attention to.

In Roman mythology, the god Janus is depicted with two heads, one looking east, the other looking west. In a sense, Jesus is asking us to have this kind of split vision. Looking one way, we honor and respect our professionalism and deal with the situation on this level. Looking the other way, we monitor our own reactions, and if we are feeling anything but peace; perceiving and feeling anything other than shared interests in terms of ourselves and the patient (even though on the bodily level there is a big difference), then we know we have to ask for help, because now we are as sick as the person whom we are trying to help. This reflects the Course's distinction between false and true empathy (T-16.I). False empathy identifies with the patient's weakness or problem (the *body*), isolating the person from others, including ourselves, by virtue of the horrific symptoms that clearly make patients and their problems unique and special. True empathy identifies with our common purpose. We empathize with the patient's *mind*, which suffers from the effects of the insane belief in separation, as we all do. This shared mind contains the weakness of the ego, the strength of the Holy Spirit, and the power to choose between them.

To digress for a moment, the pamphlet on psycho-therapy, which I mentioned before, was only half finished when I first read it. I was obviously expecting something that would talk about psychotherapy, at least as I experienced it as a therapist. Of course, it doesn't do that at all. Its focus is only on the therapist. I remember saying something to Helen to that effect, and she looked at me and said, "What else would you expect?," which of course was true. There is one line in the pamphlet that sums it up, and it is so important that the idea is repeated in the very next paragraph: "It is in the instant that the therapist forgets to judge the patient that healing occurs" (P-3.II.6:1). This says nothing about the patient, nothing about the course of psychotherapy, nothing about technique, nothing about training in the usual sense of the word. The second statement, "Yet it is when judgment ceases that healing occurs…" (P-3.II.7:1), means that therapists with healed minds do not see their patients as separate from themselves. When we see someone who has a profound neurosis or brain injury, it is tempting to see a difference and judge that difference, even if it is a benign judgment: "Oh you poor dear, let me help you."

When the therapist forgets to judge, forgets to see separate interests and sees only the sameness of the mind, that is healing and true empathy. As a therapist, or healer in any shape or form, professional or not, when you find yourself making a judgment that the person sitting across from you is different (not in form which is obvious, but in content), you realize that your mind is unhealed and you are an unhealed healer. At that point, anything you do will be contaminated by what is unhealed in you, which is the belief that separation is real, made serious by your sleeping guilt and misperception of your patient. This is false empathy. Being a psychotherapist, neuro-psychologist or any other role has as its sole purpose learning to heal your mind through that form, which means it is the opportunity to undo your belief in guilt. If you do not see it that way, you will be caught in specialness and will think you are doing something important, significant, and healing. What, then, is to be done? There is nothing to be done. Healing has already occurred and needs only to be accepted.

Q: Does that mean that once therapists have healed their own minds, they are not helpful to anyone?

A: No. Actually, it is only then that the therapist begins to be really helpful. On a practical level, you don't take your shingle down. After all, you still have to eat. Your healed mind deepens the level of healing, healing on eight burners instead of four. The love in your healed mind now can flow through you without impediment.

6. Discussion

Q: One of the hard parts about what you are saying is when you are quoting the line that talks about judgment ("Healing occurs when the therapist forgets to judge his patient."), I think of judgment as condemnation. My typical reaction is, "What a horrible situation you've been through," and I feel very bad for them. I know that is a judgment and false empathy. They are suffering through a horrible situation, as are their families.

A: On a human level it is very hard not to feel that. You do not want to become cold and insensitive, but at the same time you want to respect people's pain as they are experiencing it, and you also do not want to lose sight of the fact that the real problem is the ego. You have to be really careful that you do not cross that line and become callous and insensitive. Yet, for your own healing, you need to realize that the patient has chosen that. Everything is a script, and as the Course says, we are "reviewing mentally what has gone by" (W-pI.158.4:5).

If something is happening in my life, I chose it. It does not make me responsible for your ego. If I have just been raped by you, it does not mean that I am responsible for your attack on me. But it does mean that I am responsible for how I look at this. And if all this has already happened, and I am "reviewing mentally what has gone by," why did I choose to review this again? There are always and only two reasons: the ego delights in my once again being an innocent victim, while to the Holy Spirit it is another opportunity for me finally to learn the lesson that I am not the effect of someone else's sin ("I am not the victim of the world I see." [W-pI.31]). No matter what happens to my body or the bodies of my loved ones, I can still be at peace. I am in control of my mind. I am not in control of the world and cannot control other people, but I can control my mind. Lesson 34, "I could see peace instead of this," is one of those really important lessons. No matter what has happened to my body, whether I am a quadraplegic because of a bomb that exploded in Iraq, or something terrible has happened to my family, I, the healed mind, can still be peaceful.

The real help would be some response on the part of the therapist—it does not have to be verbal—that allows me, if not today, perhaps tomorrow (W-pI. 124.10:1), to learn that I can be peaceful instead. I do not have to be angry. I do not have to feel that my life is shattered because my body has been shattered. If I am a professional who is confronting a person in this situation, at the same time that I am commiserating with the person's pain and the unfairness of what has happened on one level, on a deeper level of my mind I want to be peaceful enough to say and mean, by my demonstration, "You can learn the lesson of being peaceful." How you communicate that happy lesson relates to your skill as a therapist. Once again, I am certainly not talking about being callous and insensitive, nor hitting people over the head with metaphysical principles. But to be truly helpful means to help people in pain recognize on some level that this is a classroom they have chosen in order to learn that regardless of what has been done to the body, peace is a decision they can make.

Imagine the incalculable benefit for suffering people to learn the lesson that will free them from the dream of brokenness and pain! Feeling sorry for them and reinforcing the fact that they are victims, while on the one hand may make them feel good and loved at the moment, will not help them awaken from the dream. And if that is your goal for yourself, why would that not be your goal for someone else? Again, I am not talking about what you verbally say, and I am certainly not saying you should be unkind and insensitive to other people anymore than I would say you should go to a funeral and laugh and say, "What death? What body in a coffin?" That is not helpful. But in your mind you know, because you are a mind that yearns to be healed of the source of all pain.

This is why you have to understand this from the perspective of the mind above the battleground, a mind that is choosing the world it experiences. The Course says "no one dies without his own consent" (W-pI.152.1:4). It is likewise true that no one has an accident without his own consent, or boards an airplane that is going to crash without his own consent. This is not the consent of the person as a body, but as a decision-making mind. I cannot emphasize enough that you will not learn this course and understand it if you read it as a body. It can be understood only as a mind. Again, that is the crucial distinction between false and true empathy: the former perceives special bodies; the latter sees only the shared mind that has chosen pain instead of the joy of God (W-pI.190).

A line from the workbook, if taken out of context, sounds horrific, saying that those who understand what forgiving means will "laugh at pain and loss, at sickness and at grief, at poverty, starvation and at death" (W-pI.187.6:4). This is not horrific when you understand its context; in fact, the words "gentle laughter" occur after that. On the level of the healed mind, we would laugh at the silliness of believing that God's Son could be hurt in any way, shape, or form. How could what God created be hurt? What God did *not* create can indeed be hurt, because the thought that created him, or miscreated him, was a thought of hurt. However, the purpose of this course is to teach us we are minds, and what better way to teach and to learn than to be involved in a profession that deals with broken physical and emotional bodies?

So often the question is asked, how can I be a doctor, work in an emergency room, etc., and practice this course that says I am not a body? How could I be a juror, lawyer, judge, or participate in any other part of a system that is all about judgment, when the course says that I should not judge? Nevertheless, that is the perfect place to be so you can learn and teach what it means to be without judgment. Being in a hospital is a perfect place to learn that you are not a body and other people are not bodies. It is the perfect classroom because in the midst of the psychological and physical pain, your being peaceful and truly present to all those who suffer, patients and staff alike, teaches a wonderful lesson. You are helping them to build a foundation, so that when the time comes that they can really learn they are not bodies, they will learn it. Your example of defenselessness and kindness is what helps them reach that point. That is the foundation. You want people to learn by your example that regardless of their situation they can still be peaceful, and therefore are not justified in feeling unfairly treated or victimized. From the world's point of view, many people are clearly justified in feeling this way, but you want to help them leave that world. You want to help them remember they are a mind. Minds cannot hurt or be hurt. They cannot attack or be attacked. Only bodies can.

To state this again, what you want to do when you are in a situation where people are in pain—whether physical, emotional, financial, marital, parental, or whatever the seeming source—is to be an example of someone who is at peace, who is above the battleground looking down, which means that you are unaffected by what the world is doing. You may seem to be affected, and you often need to interact with people on the level they can accept, which is simple kindness expressed in a form the person can understand without fear (see T-2.IV.5). But if you truly want to be kind, you can be so only as a healed mind. You cannot be kind as a body. Bodies are never kind, since they only look out for themselves and their multitudinous needs. Sympathizing with certain people is never kind, because that excludes others. This means you are reinforcing separation and differentiation, the ego's bread and butter. That is not helpful, nor is it truly kind.

And so, if you want to be helpful, you have to be part of the help, part of your own healing. Recall, "It is in the instant the therapist forgets to judge the patient that healing occurs." Judgment always means separation, specialness, and differentiation (false empathy). Vision is all-inclusive and sees everyone as the same (true empathy). This is the only way you will find peace, the only way you will be lifted out of the dream and help other people be lifted out of the same dream of separation and pain. The healed mind does not make the error real. It may sound as if you are by your behavior, but your mind remains centered on the truth. The basic message of this course, the message of every form of the universal course, is that "God's Son is guiltless…" (M-1.3:5). If you are guiltless there is nothing to project. With nothing to project, there is no body: no pain, suffering, loss, or death. No matter what happens to your body, the love in your mind has not been lost. That is the lesson you want to teach: "God's Son is guiltless. You are guiltless, and everyone else is as well."

The lesson I just cited, Lesson 190, says, "If God is real, there is no pain. If pain is real, there is no God" (W-pI.190.3:3-4). You do not want to reinforce people's pain. That does not mean you do not work with them on the level of their pain to help them be released from it, but in your healed mind you know the only pain is believing you have separated from your Creator. That belief is the only pain, and the source of all pain.

The reason we cling to pain, therefore, is that it proves there is no God. How could perfect Love have pain? How could we who are part of perfect Love experience pain? If we experience pain, or identify with other people's experience of pain, it is because we want to deny God and His perfect Love. It works very nicely for the ego when I am attacked and can suffer. But if we want to learn the lesson that we are guiltless, along with everyone else, we must demonstrate it. We want to live in a world of guilt, brokenness, pain, and suffering so we can learn this world of guilt has no power over the love and peace in our mind. In summary, then, when we deal with a broken body, psyche, or bank account, we want to demonstrate the healing thought in our minds that God's Son remains in the love and peace in which he was created. We demonstrate this by having our peace be unchanged—before, during, and after our encounter with another's pain and suffering. And so we reinforce what we are demonstrating, learning guiltlessness as we teach it is how our unhealed minds are healed.

The central idea of the power of our minds to choose is reinforced when we consider that when we make other people's suffering real, we ultimately condemn them to being a body, making it impossible to respect the power of their decision-making minds to choose differently. We can feel people's pain, but on another level we want to realize that their minds chose that. If we truly love and care about them, we want to reinforce the power of their minds to choose to be at peace. We cannot do that if we remain part of their dreams of pain and suffering.

This is a very difficult lesson, to be sure. You know the point I made earlier that this is a very difficult course. No matter how many times Jesus says it is simple, it is difficult because its *only* emphasis is that we are minds, and what it means to be a mind is that we have the power to choose a different teacher. That is the core of Jesus' teaching. This entire course is based on that. Don't let anyone tell you anything else.

106

It is only about regaining the mind's decision-making power. That is why over and over again we are told to choose. At the very end of the text comes "Choose Once Again" (T-31.VIII). Even midst our living in a world of war and suffering, we want to remember we are a mind that can decide to be at peace.

If you find yourself feeling sorry for people who are suffering, which is a normal thing to feel, you are but reinforcing the fact that we are not minds, but bodies, and that the separation actually happened. It is a most difficult lesson, but its value cannot be overestimated. The reason we are here is to learn that we are not here. The Course says, "How else can you find joy in a joyless place except by realizing that you are not there?" (T-6.II.6:1). That is what this is saying. How do you find joy in a place that is filled with such pain and suffering, "a dry and dusty world, where starved and thirsty creatures come to die" (W-pII.13.5:1)? This *is* this world, and it is not a joyful place. How do you find joy here? By realizing that the world has never left its source in the illusory mind, and therefore is not real. Learning that is true joy.

But where are you? In your mind. *A Course in Miracles* is all about the mind—*mind, mind, mind*. The Bible and Jesus' gospel teachings are all about the body—*body, body, body*. This book is only about the mind. The challenge, therefore, is to be present to people's bodily suffering, emotionally and physically, to be kind to them and meet their needs on the level they can accept, yet knowing that the real suffering is found in the mind's decision for guilt. And because the mind decided for guilt, it can easily decide for innocence. This is the truth you want to demonstrate to the sick and suffering, demonstrated not by what you say or do, but by how you are. You demonstrate that the decision you made for the Holy Spirit as your Teacher they can make, too; the same decision you made to remember you are a mind who can choose peace instead of conflict, they can make as well.

That is how you help. Indeed, it is the only way you can help, which is why Jesus told Helen not to ask him to take her fear away, because that was not the problem and would not be helpful. It would depreciate, denigrate, dismiss, and render powerless the only thing in the universe that could help her: the mind's power to choose. Therefore, we want to hold ourselves up as examples of having chosen to be above the battleground as healed minds. And then, most important of all, to be patient with ourselves when we become afraid and flee back to the body.

Concern for a Family Member's Illness

Q: My sister is severely mentally ill, and I can almost never talk about her without crying. Just to see her is very painful. Today, though, after reading the line from the text that says in our suffering of any kind we see our concealed desire to kill (T-31.V.15:10), I began to make a connection between that and my suffering because of my sister's illness. I probably have gotten a whole lot of mileage out of her illness, but I don't really know how to grieve it in a way that actually helps me get past it. There is a lot of mental illness in my family, not just her, and it has always been my big fear that I would become ill, too. I don't know how to bring those two together. There is a part of me that feels that I have been grieving long enough and yet it is still really raw. Is that passage saying that my suffering reflects a desire to kill her? To blame my family? To blame my parents? Can you help me understand how the Course would see this?

A: You would have to be willing to look at the situation differently from the way you have looked at it all your life. You have seen your sister throughout your life as different from you, while also harboring the fear that you will end up not being different, that you will end up suffering from mental illness, too. As long as you see yourself as daughter in your family and sister to your siblings, there is no way out of it. The only way out would be, as the Course says, to raise yourself above the battleground (T-23.IV) and to understand the purpose behind what you are feeling.

The truth of the matter is that you are all thoughts in a mind; and as thoughts in a mind, you are all perfect. Your sister represents a distortion of that perfect thought by being imperfect in form. It does not matter whether it is a mental illness or a congenital physical illness—the challenge is not to see her as different. Your saying that you are tired of feeling this way is really important. In a sense, that is what the invitation to the Holy Spirit or Jesus is. We have to say, enough already! The Course says early in the text that everyone's tolerance for pain is high, but we all reach a point where we say "there *must* be a better way" (T-2.III.3). It sounds as if you are nearing that point.

The "better way" is to realize that, first, this is a dream of the unhealed mind that your family has shared, including your sister, and that the ego lesson is that it makes the world and suffering real; it makes differences and unfair treatment real. The correction for that is to realize this is a classroom in which to learn that your sister is as perfect as you are, as are your parents, your brother, or anyone else.

The most difficult part of this correction process is to realize that you have an investment in seeing her this way, and yourself as the innocent victim. Even harder is realizing that the sadness that you feel that makes it impossible for you to even think of her or speak about her without crying, is showing your concealed desire to kill, just as you were saying, and that you have an investment in seeing her this way. The tears and the suffering are a way to disguise that by saying this is really upsetting to you.

The ultimate thought at the bottom of this, which would help you get beyond it once and for all, is that *you want her to be this way.* You know, there is that terrible Christian line, "There but for the grace of God go I." If, as the ego claims, it is *one or the other*, then you are the healthy one; she is the sick one. You want her to be ill so that you do not have to be. She needs to be sacrificed so you can be saved from God's wrath. That is the real value. The fear, though, is that you will be found out and then punished by being made ill the same way—you will end up mentally ill, too. But your fear that you will become mentally ill is not the reality. The thought that would really help you, which I think is the linchpin that holds all this together, is, again, that *you want her to be this way.* Thus, your feeling guilty that you are not ill the way your sister is hides the "real" guilt, which is that you want her to be that way; her illness is your secret wish. That is the source of your tears.

Q: It is exhausting to discuss this.

A: Yes, that is because you do not want to let it go. In a sense, your whole lifetime is built on the fact that you are the favored one. You are not sick—she is sick. I frequently quote the line from the *Psychotherapy* pamphlet, "And who could weep but for his innocence?" (P-2.IV.1:7). Your tears are coming from your guilt that you have thrown your innocence away by pretending that you are innocent and your sister is guilty; she is the sick one, not you. The source of the tears is that somehow you will be found out again, that you are not as innocent as you appear to be.

The bottom line in your healing would be to see the investment you have in seeing her this way and always having seen her this way. What will save you—the way to enter God's Presence—is to realize you and your sister are the same, not in the form of mental illness, but because you are thoughts of the same mind. That would help you begin the process of letting go of the investment in seeing her this way. Then the nightmare will be over, and your mind will be healed of the mental illness we all suffer from: guilt.

That is a good example, actually, of seeing how you want to get beyond the perception and experience of differences to see the universal sameness. You cannot do that as a body, though. You can do that only as a mind. And that is the way that you will remember God.

Application to Animals and Pets

Q: I am a veterinarian and I work with animals. Is it appropriate to approach this pretty much the same way with animals? I know when I am examining an animal I feel I am connecting with that pet's mind. Do we assume they have the same type of a framework, that it is their minds' decision to suffer?

A: Absolutely! There is a passage that comes in the form of a prayer, saying, "How holy is the smallest grain of sand, when it is recognized as being part of the completed picture of God's Son!" (T-28.IV.9:4). This has nothing to do with form. Remember what I began with: *form and content*. Homo sapiens is a form as lifeless as this lectern, watch, or book. The first law of chaos is that there is a hierarchy of illusions. That same section, from which I quoted the part about painting rosy lips upon a skeleton, says, "There is no life outside of Heaven" (T-23.II.19:1). In the arrogance of our madness, we think there is a distinction between animate and inanimate. Imagine the absurdity of that. We actually think there is a difference. "There is no life outside of Heaven." There can be no hierarchy of illusions. Nothing is alive here. As an adult attending a puppet show with a little child, you know that the table, chair, and puppet that is sitting in the chair are all the same. There is no difference among them for they are only different pieces of wood carved in different ways, dressed differently, painted differently. This is how Jesus looks at all this.

Thus, it makes no difference whether you are ministering to an animal, person, plant, car, or rock, because it is all about you. It is all about what you have chosen in your mind and that you project onto the animal, person, plant, car, or rock. There is nothing outside you, which is why there is no hierarchy of illusions—an illusion is an illusion is an illusion. The smallest grain of sand is a projection of the mind's thought of separation. How can it be different from a complex mammal? This is a difficult course because on every page Jesus is saying this to us. There is nothing outside your mind. The world is nothing more or less than a projected dream.

When you go to a movie and see the different images on the screen, is any one image more alive than any other—whether it be a man, woman, or child; animal, monster, or object? Is there really any difference? They are all an illusion, projections of a film that runs through a projector. There are no people in the projection booth that you see on the screen. What we see is only the projected and illusory film. You would not make a distinction about what is alive or not alive on the screen. So why do we do it here? This is a screen, too; a screen onto which we project a decision of one of two thought systems, the wrong- or right-minded one. It is this simplicity of choice that leads Jesus to say that his course is simple and easy. There is nothing but these two alternatives.

When you are right-minded, you are peaceful no matter where you are, what you are doing, or whom you are with. Everything is the same. It does not matter what the symptoms are that confront you. Everything and everyone is the same because everyone and everything is an illusion. You are projecting what is within you. "Projection makes perception"

6. Discussion

(T-21.in.1). The unhealed healer thinks there are situations and problems out there that require intervention. At that point it is the unhealed healers who need intervention, needing to be reminded that they are minds, and that "I could see peace instead of this," regardless of what is going on in bodies.

Should There Be a Change in the Patient's Condition?

Q: If we are able to bring the illusion to truth, wouldn't we expect that patient to be helped?

A: Of course.

Q: Well I don't mean just on a spiritual level, but wouldn't we expect them to be relieved of their symptoms?

A: Absolutely not. Let me elaborate. It depends on how you define sickness. If you define sickness as a symptom, then what alleviates the symptom would be what the Course calls "magic," which is anything other than a change of mind. This would include medicine (chemical or natural), laying on of hands, saying prayers, standing upside-down, taking a cold shower, hot shower, or no shower—anything you believe would be helpful.

If, however, you define sickness as guilt, or more specifically the decision to be guilty, which is the decision to separate, the solution is to undo the belief in separation. If you are a cancer patient and I am the doctor, nurse, practitioner of any kind, a friend or family member, and I do not experience myself as separate from you, I am giving you the message that we are not separated. In addition, my defenselessness is saying that you can make the same right-minded decision I did. At that point the sickness is healed.

Your question is, "What about the symptom?" If the cause of the symptoms is guilt, and if the patient has undone guilt in the holy instant, the symptoms would disappear, *assuming that the symptoms came from guilt*. But although the patient's mind is healed in this holy instant, it may be unhealed in the next moment. The fact that my mind is healed now does not mean my patients have totally accepted the healing. I cannot accept the healing for them, but can only remind them of their mind's power to choose peace or conflict. My representing the Holy Spirit because my mind is healed does not mean they necessarily have accepted Him too. If people are still afraid of healing, they would step aside from it and the symptoms would continue. In my healed mind, however, they are no longer sick. Although they may still have the symptoms, I know they are healed because they are. I am inviting those who suffer to join in my happy dream of forgiveness and healing. If I become concerned because symptoms remain, they are inviting me to join in their dream of sickness, and I am joining them.

Q: What comes up for me in response to that is that if you right-mindedly deal with the illusion, there is no longer a separate mind deciding on its own to be sick or not.

A: That is correct. My healed mind knows better. But you still have the freedom to choose not to identify with the healed mind. While I know that you are not sick, if you are not willing at this point to accept the healing and accept that what the right mind is saying is true, you will deny the healing. By the same token, we would all agree that Jesus accepted the Atonement. That may be all well and good for him, we would say, but we still feel we are bodies stuck here, still getting sick and becoming angry, growing old and dying. But his mind is healed. Well, our minds are healed, too, except we are still choosing against the healing.

On an individual level this means that if I am with you and you are sick, and I do not see that as your reality because we are the same (without at the same time denying the presence of symptoms within the dream), in that holy instant my mind is healed. Your mind must be healed, too, since minds are joined. Despite this truth, you have the freedom not to accept it, just as we all have the freedom not to accept what is written in the Course. We may know it is true, but there remains a part of us, the ego, that still says: "I choose to keep this at arm's length to preserve my separated self, even though these healing words come from a source that sees us only as one.

Q: I would think that seeing the truth at that level would trump the illusion.

A: Yes, if your mind is healed, but there is yet a part of you that fears the truth. And so you hold the healing off because you know that if you accept it, everything about your ego, everything special with which you identify, is false. This could lead you to sincerely say, "I am not quite ready for this yet."

6. Discussion

Q: What do you think is happening with people who do spiritual healing, like in Christian Science? They have a similar approach where the practitioner doesn't treat the patients, who treat themselves by seeing the illusion.

A: Yes. They could be very good at using their minds to change the course of a physical illness and undo the symptoms, but if they are not undoing guilt, then they and their patients are still sick. This is a different view of sickness. Christian Science, as an example, certainly teaches that sickness is of the mind. But they do not say that sickness is separation the way *A Course in Miracles* does, and they do not speak about the identification with guilt. And certainly they do not really deal with our resistance to accepting the truth of the mind's power.

Many people are quite adept at demonstrating that the mind is more powerful than the body. Long years of practice and discipline can help you to stay under water for 30 minutes, walk on burning coals, and levitate. But none of this will bring you closer to Heaven. Showing that the mind is more powerful than the body can be impressive, and even helpful, but it does not undo guilt. This is a course in using the power of the mind to undo the ego thought system, not to manipulate the external world, which only makes the error real.

Q: It seems like not so much a course in one or the other. It is more that as one develops more closeness to truth and more insight, there should be some perceived effect in terms of there being less illusion around you. As a veterinarian, I see nothing but suffering and disease, at the same time I am working on enlightenment for myself. It seems like I should see improvement, a happier dream all around me.

A: You are defining "the happy dream" as the amelioration of the physical symptoms. *A Course in Miracles* defines it as peace. Yes, what you are saying would make sense if you redefined your expectations; i.e., if your mind is healed, or you are on the road to becoming healed, the perceived effects would be that you become more peaceful, kind, and loving, and less judgmental, angry, and depressed. People around you, then, would experience this from you, and that would be a call that invites them, likewise, to become more peaceful and less angry.

It takes two people to have a fight. If someone is angry, anxious, or guilty and you do not participate in that, you are undoing the separation and therefore undoing the war or battle. Sure, over time you would expect people who live with you, work with you, etc., including the animals who are ill, to be more peaceful. But that does not necessarily mean they would always accept that peace, nor does it mean they would accept the peace that could help them undo their mind's belief in illness.

From the point of view of *A Course in Miracles*, you are getting caught in the level confusion that "makes the error real." You demand witnesses to the Course's efficacy and your work with it in terms of something changing externally. Some of this confusion relates to what Jesus means by our being responsible. On the level of the collective mind, we are all, as one Son, responsible for the material world we made together. But that is hardly helpful to us as we experience our lives as individual persons. What *is* helpful, however, is to know that we are responsible for *how* we see the world—does it make us happy or sad, peaceful or conflicted?

As I said before, it is absolutely essential, even if at first it is not your experience, that you read *A Course in Miracles* from the perspective of mind and not the personal world of your body. Otherwise, you will surely misunderstand the Course and distort its teachings. Jesus is never talking about the body.

Let me read an important passage in this regard. It is from "The Responsibility for Sight":

> This is the only thing that you need do for vision, happiness, release from pain and complete escape from sin, all to be given you. Say only this, but mean it with no reservations, for here the power of salvation lies:
>
> *I **am** responsible for what I see.*
> *I choose the feelings I experience, and I decide upon the goal I would achieve.*
> *And everything that seems to happen to me I ask for, and receive as I have asked* (T-21.II.2:1-5).

If you read this carelessly, you would think Jesus is saying you are responsible for what you see in front of you. Again, that is not his point and is certainly not helpful. How could guilt not follow from seeing all the suffering and tragedy in the world around us? Remember that *perception is interpretation*. It is not *what* my eyes see that I am responsible for (physical symptoms, for example) but the *way* I see—*perception is interpretation*.

The clear implication is that I am responsible for how I see my patients. "*I choose the feelings I experience*": When I am with those who suffer, am I guilty, anxious, fearful, or depressed, feeling responsible for

123

their condition or its lack of amelioration? Or am I feeling peaceful? *"I decide upon the goal I would achieve"*: Is my goal that physical symptoms be alleviated, or is my goal the peace of God? Remember the line, "...seek not to change the world, but choose to change your mind about the world" (T-21.in.1:7). Regardless of my role, I am not here to seek change in my patients' symptoms; but rather to change my mind about their symptoms, not give them power to affect my inner peace.

Please remember that we are not talking about behavior. Obviously if you are a physician, a veterinarian, anyone in any helping profession, you want to help, and you should use your training and expertise to be helpful on the physical or psychological level. But we are talking about an attitude; not what you do, but with whom you do it, the ego or the Holy Spirit. *"And everything that seems to happen to me I ask for, and receive as I have asked"*: What is it that seems to happen to me? People treat me unfairly, persecute me, take advantage of me, abuse and victimize me. All this is made very clear in the next line:

> Deceive yourself no longer that you are helpless
> in the face of what is done to you (T-21.II.2:6).

On the level of the world, many times we are indeed "helpless in the face of what is done to [us]." If we are a prisoner of war and are tortured, there is very little we can do physically to stop what is happening. If we are in a concentration camp, there is nothing we can do to stop what is happening to us behaviorally. If we have plans for an outdoor picnic and it is stormy weather, we have no choice but to cancel our plans. Perhaps we have alternative plans, but we certainly cannot have the picnic outdoors.

Jesus is focusing on our feelings of helplessness: *"Deceive yourself no longer that you are helpless in the face of what is done to you."* My body may be helpless, but my mind is all-powerful. I can choose to remain at peace regardless of my external circumstances. I could be a physician or a veterinarian, with very little I can do for the sick person or animal. I do what I can, of course, but perhaps the illness has progressed too far. Nonetheless, I can be at peace. I am not responsible for the symptoms I see in front to me, for those are their choice. But I am responsible for whether I give those symptoms power to take the peace of God from me, or give the removal of the symptoms power to make me happy and feel good about myself, saying: "Look what a wonderfully helpful person I am. I stopped the pain and cured the disease." Either way, I am giving the world power to make me happy or sad, invalidating the power of my mind to decide between genuine peace or conflict.

Clearly, then, the world has no power over me. My decision-making mind is what alone chooses my experience of peace or conflict, joy or terror. To say this one more time, I am not responsible for what you choose. I am responsible only for choosing whether I join you on the dance floor of specialness and death, where you are inviting me by being sick, fearful, or angry, or inviting you onto my dance floor with Jesus, where you and I are not separate but dance conjointly to Jesus' sweet song: *"together, or not at all"* (T-19.IV-D12:8; italics mine).

Q: One more question, please. Let's say my career has been one where every day I get up and go to work and see disease and suffering. I have assumed it comes from the ego that has made it to hold us here, to engage us in the separation. I don't want to make it too abstract, but if I am dealing with suffering, and it is not really individual because there aren't separate individuals, just one mind projecting this, what is my involvement with this? It is not something I feel I can be emotionally aloof to, and I know you weren't suggesting that. But at the same time, it does affect me. It is my reality. How can I understand disease and health in a more universal way?

A: This is a very good question, and bears on the very points I have been discussing, the place where people really get confused with the Course. Part of the confusion is the metaphysics, which tell us that all this is a collective illusion that was made as a purposive act to attack God and keep Him away. I will therefore first speak more metaphysically, and then apply this to your specific practice as a veterinarian, which we can generalize to everyone's situation.

To begin with, what confuses the issue is when we define sickness in a restricted way: the symptoms the world calls sickness or disease. However, looking at the world as *A Course in Miracles* does, understanding its origin and purpose, we realize that breathing reflects a sickness because breathing keeps this body alive. This keeps the limitation of love alive, and contributes to keeping the world in existence. This is the attack on God, and this insane thought system is the sickness.

If there is no hierarchy of illusions (the ego's first law of chaos is that there is), which is why there is *no order of difficulty in miracles*, then simply being here in a body is the sickness. Being born, let alone the mind's choosing the ego, is the sickness. It is not a specific growth on your body, not a tumor or cold, not a broken limb. The mere fact that we exist as bodies means we are sick. Well people don't come here; they stay with God. In order to address your question satisfactorily, we have to shift our perspective entirely.

Everything in the world is sick, which means everything here witnesses to the reality of the separation. The fact that I take a breath every four or eight seconds tells me that I believe I am in a constant state of lack or scarcity. If my true nature as spirit is abundance, I am saying that God is wrong because look, I have to breathe, I have to eat every few hours, not to mention all my other normal functioning as a body. All this is part of the sickness and disease, and we accomplished this as one Son. Our collective mind chose the ego and then projected its thought system as the world. Setting aside those rare people who have accepted the Atonement for themselves, all who are here are sick.

We came into this world for two reasons: As egos, we sought to prove that we are sick, separation is the reality, God is wrong and we are right, and that we are innocent victims of the world around us; as right minds, we sought to learn that we are wrong and God is right. The ego has us come here to be further immersed in the prison of its thought system, expressed in the prison of the body. The Holy Spirit, also in our minds, helps us see the world as a classroom in which we can choose a different Teacher, Who teaches us the lessons that help us leave the prison entirely. So that is our simple choice: the world as prison or classroom.

We all have our lessons. The ego speaks first, is always wrong, and the Holy Spirit is the Answer. We choose to be born into families that breed separation, and naturally then reinforce the ego thought system. We have to deal with our bodies as we grow up and mature, and that solidifies the belief in the reality of change. We become educated and learn about a world that does not exist. We graduate or not, have families or not, but we all need to have a source of money so we can continue to live. Whatever our means of support, we make the body real as well as its underlying thought of separation. And we keep going and going and going. In your particular case, you became a veterinarian, I became a psychologist, etc. We all became whatever we became, but behind it all is the need to reinforce and preserve the ego thought system that is the antithesis of Heaven and proves it wrong.

At some point we say, "There must be another way," which means whether or not I consciously articulate it, I am saying "I want another teacher to deliver me from this prison and teach me the lessons I need to learn to go home." Then your veterinarian practice, which is focused on suffering and pain, at times death, becomes a classroom in which you realize the suffering, pain, and death that your eyes see are all part of the ego's lessons in separation. The entirety of the ego thought system is caught up here: We are sinful and deserve to be punished, a punishment that culminates in suffering and death. All this reinforces the ego dream, until we ask for help from another Teacher and begin to see things differently.

We now realize that suffering is not of the body, and we reach this realization when we see our life and profession as serving a spiritual purpose. We recognize that suffering is a projection of the mind's guilt, and everything we see outside is its mirror or projection. Since we believe we are separated, we appear to deal with it as individuals. We are not yet at the point of saying everything is one. That occurs at the end when our minds are healed. We deal with what we perceive to be our unique classroom. Whether we do it as a veterinarian or therapist, we are involved with sickness, suffering, and pain. The lesson is to learn that external suffering is the mirror of the internal pain we all have, regardless of the species. We all suffer from guilt, including our patients (human and animal alike) and their families. Everyone here suffers. We are not alone and separated and are more alike than otherwise. Indeed, we are the same for we all have the same split mind.

We redefine suffering and realize we are no longer confronted with suffering that is so overwhelming that it is hard to make it through the day. We see our day as a classroom in which we learn that the external suffering is a mirror of the wrong decision everyone's mind has made. We use each day as an opportunity to learn that everyone calls out for help: the sick animals, the families that are upset, and we who are dealing with them. Everything can now shift, which means whether the symptoms disappear or not is irrelevant. On the level of form, we do whatever we can to alleviate suffering in any living thing, but remain aware that what we are really doing is withdrawing the projections we have put on our patients. We demonstrate to them that we can make a right-minded decision, and so can they. This is accomplished simply by being defenseless and kind. We do what we can for the physical pain, but in our minds we know that what we are really doing is alleviating the mind's pain, the real cause of the suffering.

After the Mind Is Healed

Q: Just so I have something to look forward to in the future, when you are above all this and in that state, is there something in the Course I can read that describes what we will experience, what we have to look forward to?

A: Yes, and there are several beautiful sections that describe this, such as "Where Sin Has Left," "The Forgotten Song," and "The Forgiven World."

Q: So there is still a world out there?

A: Indeed. When you are above the battleground in your mind, everything is different. That is when the world looks different, not because the forms change, but because *you* have changed. When that change becomes permanent, you are in what *A Course in Miracles* calls *the real world*. Again, the world does not change externally, but your perception changes.

From that healed perception, a peace will come that will never leave, and its gentleness will embrace *all* things, animate and inanimate alike.

Saying No

Q: What do you do if you are being called on all day for help? Things can get out of hand if at some point you don't say no or place limits.

A: What you describe as getting out of hand is the world of form. There is nothing in *A Course in Miracles* that says you should hear and answer every call for help on the level of form. In fact, Jesus once told Helen, in the context of a public figure who made this mistake, that people who are unable to leave the requests of others unanswered have not escaped ego-centricity. Jesus added that he never made that mistake and he asked Helen not to make it either. His point was that if we are unable to say no on the level of form, it is the ego talking. Behind that inability is the thought that we are the saviors of the world, and all the people who call upon us need our help. And if we do not save them, they will suffer and it will be our fault. We would have failed not only them but the holy mission that God gave us. Implicit in Jesus' words to

Helen was that she should ask him before deciding to help or not. This way we will never feel we are badgered ceaselessly, that people are trying to get something from us. We cannot help, then, but feel sacrificial, resentful, and exhausted. And so, again, the crucial difference is between form (the body's behavior) and content (the mind's decision for its teacher).

We should always answer another's call for help on the level of content (being kind and defenseless), but that does not always mean on the level of form. Since we are not the ones who could know, we need to ask the one who does. This means that we have to be free of the investment of seeing people in need, or not seeing them—the same difference. On the one hand I want to say yes to everyone because that proves I am a good person. On the other hand, I do not want to talk to anyone because I have more important things to do and do not want to be bothered. The issue always comes down to the same thing. If I truly want to ask for help—what I should do or not do—I need to ask for help of my teacher to get the interference of guilt out of the way so I can receive the loving answer *that is already there*. We cannot heal others unless we are healed ourselves. Only then do we truly know that there was never anything to be healed. We have merely accepted the truth that Heaven's love is our reality, a love that is freely shared with *all* God's creation once we have accepted it is our own.

Closing:

"And now in all your doings be you blessed."

We close this book with the end of the manual for teachers (M-29.8). All four books of *A Course in Miracles* (including the clarification of terms) end very beautifully, and in verse. This poem that concludes the manual is a lovely expression of the healed healers we are to become. Joining with each other and with Jesus has undone our mind's belief in separation, brought on by its mistaken choice for the ego.

This, then, is Jesus' prayer for us and to us. His love that has healed our unhealed minds now extends through us into a world that does not know it. Living his love through our demonstration, we become his joyful messengers of salvation:

And now in all your doings be you blessed.
God turns to you for help to save the world.
Teacher of God, His thanks He offers you,
And all the world stands silent in the grace
You bring from Him. You are the Son He loves,
And it is given you to be the means
Through which His Voice is heard around the world,
To close all things of time; to end the sight
Of all things visible; and to undo
All things that change. Through you is ushered in
A world unseen, unheard, yet truly there.
Holy are you, and in your light the world
Reflects your holiness, for you are not
Alone and friendless. I give thanks for you,
And join your efforts on behalf of God,
Knowing they are on my behalf as well,
And for all those who walk to God with me.

AMEN

INDEX OF REFERENCES TO *A COURSE IN MIRACLES*

text

text (continued)

text (continued)

workbook for students

workbook for students (continued)

manual for teachers

manual for teachers (continued)

clarification of terms

Foundation for A COURSE IN MIRACLES®

Kenneth Wapnick received his Ph.D. in Clinical Psychology in 1968 from Adelphi University. He was a close friend and associate of Helen Schucman and William Thetford, the two people whose joining together was the immediate stimulus for the scribing of A COURSE IN MIRACLES. Kenneth has been involved with A COURSE IN MIRACLES since 1973, writing, teaching, and integrating its principles with his practice of psychotherapy. He is on the Executive Board of the Foundation for Inner Peace, publishers of A COURSE IN MIRACLES.

In 1983, with his wife Gloria, he began the Foundation for A COURSE IN MIRACLES, and in 1984 this evolved into a Teaching and Healing Center in Crompond, New York, which was quickly outgrown. In 1988 they opened the Academy and Retreat Center in upstate New York. In 1995 they began the Institute for Teaching Inner Peace through A COURSE IN MIRACLES, an educational corporation chartered by the New York State Board of Regents. In 2001 the Foundation moved to Temecula, California. The Foundation publishes a quarterly newsletter, "The Lighthouse," which is available free of charge. The following is Kenneth and Gloria's vision of the Foundation.

In our early years of studying *A Course in Miracles,* as well as teaching and applying its principles in our respective professions of psychotherapy, and teaching and school administration, it seemed evident that this was not the simplest of thought systems to understand. This was so not only in the intellectual grasp of its teachings, but perhaps more importantly in the application of these teachings to our personal lives. Thus, it appeared to us from the beginning that the Course lent itself to teaching, parallel to the ongoing teachings of the Holy Spirit in the daily opportunities within our relationships, which are discussed in the early pages of the manual for teachers.

One day several years ago while Helen Schucman and I (Kenneth) were discussing these ideas, she shared a vision that she had had of a teaching center as a white temple with a gold cross atop it. Although it was clear that this image was symbolic, we understood it to be representative of what the teaching center was to be: a place where the person of Jesus and his message in *A Course in Miracles* would be manifest. We have sometimes seen an image of a lighthouse shining its light into the sea, calling to it those passers-by who sought it. For us, this light is the Course's teaching of forgiveness, which we would hope to share with those who are drawn to the Foundation's form of teaching and its vision of *A Course in Miracles*.

This vision entails the belief that Jesus gave the Course at this particular time in this particular form for several reasons. These include:

1) the necessity of healing the mind of its belief that attack is salvation; this is accomplished through forgiveness, the undoing of our belief in the reality of separation and guilt.

2) emphasizing the importance of Jesus and/or the Holy Spirit as our loving and gentle Teacher, and developing a personal relationship with this Teacher.

3) correcting the errors of Christianity, particularly where it has emphasized suffering, sacrifice, separation, and sacrament as being inherent in God's plan for salvation.

Our thinking has always been inspired by Plato (and his mentor Socrates), both the man and his teachings. Plato's Academy was a place where serious and thoughtful people came to study his philosophy in an atmosphere conducive to their learning, and then returned to their professions to implement what they were taught by the great philosopher. Thus, by integrating abstract philosophical ideals with experience, Plato's school seemed to be the perfect model for the teaching center that we directed for so many years.

We therefore see the Foundation's principal purpose as being to help students of *A Course in Miracles* deepen their understanding of its thought system, conceptually and experientially, so that they may be more effective instruments of Jesus' teaching in their own lives. Since teaching forgiveness without experiencing it is empty, one of the Foundation's specific goals is to help facilitate the process whereby people may be better able to know that their own sins are forgiven and that they are truly loved by God. Thus is the Holy Spirit able to extend His Love through them to others.

Foundation for A Course in Miracles®

Temecula, California

Please see our Web site, www.facim.org, for a complete listing of publications and available translations. You may also write, or call our office for information:

Foundation for *A COURSE IN MIRACLES*®
41397 Buecking Drive
Temecula, CA 92590
(951) 296-6261 • fax (951) 296-5455